ARE YOU REALLY
BORN AGAIN?

ARE YOU REALLY
BORN AGAIN?

UNDERSTANDING TRUE AND FALSE CONVERSION

Kent Philpott

Earthen Vessel
Publishing

EVANGELICAL PRESS

 EVANGELICAL PRESS

 Earthen Vessel
Publishing

Evangelical Press
Faverdale North, Darlington
DL3 0PH England
Evangelical Press USA
PO Box 825, Webster NY 14580 USA
email: sales@evangelical-press.org
www.evangelicalpress.org

Earthen Vessel Publishing
289 Miller Avenue,
Mill Valley, CA 94941 USA
www.earthenvessel.net

Co-published by Evangelical Press and Earthen Vessel Publishing
First published 1998 (ISBN 0 85234 405 8)
Second revised edition 2005 (ISBN 0 85234 604 2)

All scripture quotations, unless otherwise indicated, are taken from the Holy
Bible, New International Version. Copyright 1973, 1978, 1984, International
Bible Society. Used by permission of the Hodder Headline Group. All rights
reserved.

Scripture quotations in Appendix I ('The theology of new birth' by Jonathan
Dickinson) are from the Authorized (King James) Version.

British Library Cataloguing in Publication Data available

ISBN 0 85234 604 2

To preachers of the gospel
— *and we are all preachers of the gospel*

How, then, can they call on the one they have not believed in? And how can they believe in the one of whom they have not heard? And how can they hear without someone preaching to them? (Rom. 10:14)

CONTENTS

Foreword to the second edition   ix
Preface   xiii

Introduction   1

1 Christianization or conversion?   11
2 The mystery of conversion   19
3 True conversion   25
4 Conversion: the objective facts   33
5 Conversion: the subjective experience 43
6 Signs of the converted   51
7 False conversion: a biblical basis   61
8 How do false conversions occur?   69
9 Experiences typical of true and false conversions 85
10 Signs of the unconverted   91
11 The stages of conversion   107
12 Profiles of true and false conversions 115
13 Assurance of salvation   125
14 Jacob becomes Israel: a symbol of conversion 135

Appendix I: 'The theology of new birth' 139
    by Jonathan Dickinson
Appendix II: The conversion of C. H. Spurgeon 153
    (in his own words)
Appendix III: Responses from readers of 157
    the first edition

FOREWORD
TO THE SECOND EDITION

In May 2000 I reached the age of sixty-five and felt it right to lay down my responsibilities as pastor of Great Hollands Free Church in Bracknell, England. There were a good number of unsaved friends of mine present at my farewell service. Copies of my books were on sale but the book that I urged all of my friends to buy was *Are you really born again?* by Kent Philpott. I felt that this practical book dealt with the most vital question of all at that hour; I still think it does.

Most of us regularly come across various types of people who say that they are Christians. There are those who are confident of their salvation because they have made some kind of decision to follow Christ and there are others who hope they are born again but remain full of doubts and fears.

Reading this book would particularly help the first kind of people. So many people have prayed the 'sinner's prayer' and they have been told that they are now Christians because they have done so. They do not realize that quite often all that has happened is that they have made a decision, but then when things get tough, or they find the people in their church do not live up to their expectations, they can 'unmake' that decision — and drift away from God and the people of God.

Kent maintains that such actions are not necessarily true conversions; these people may merely have changed their minds. If they were really saved when they 'asked Jesus to come into their hearts' it was not because of anything they did; it was as a result of what Christ has done on the cross. There has been a sovereign work of saving power in their lives.

Then there are the other types of people who truly *are* born again but because of their personality or a particular circumstance of life they have doubts about it. They think they are not *good* enough for God to have mercy on them and grant them his salvation. Or they may think they are not *bad* enough to be given such a blessing. They may have read or heard a glowing testimony of someone who was saved from a life steeped in sin — a womanizer, a gambler, a drunkard or a drug addict. And because they have never succumbed to such evils, they think they are too ordinary to be saved. These people would also find much to help them in this book.

Sadly, in these days, there are comparatively few professions of conversions in Britain but the opposite is true in some parts of the world. But whether there are few or many claims of salvation it is vital that they prove to be genuine. One test that the Lord Jesus Christ gave in John 15:8 was that they 'bear much fruit, showing [themselves] to be [his] disciples'.

Kent is concerned that those who claim to be real Christians should know for certain that they are born again. This small book sets it all down in fine clarity. Its great benefit is that its short chapters are simply written so that the evidences of true conversion, as well as the signs of false conversion, are clearly detailed.

So, whether you are seeking salvation yourself, struggling with your own faith or seeking to help other people along their Christian pathway, you will find much spiritual guidance in this volume. I would have appreciated this book when I was a young pastor but now, as I approach my seventies, I find it a blessing to my own soul, as well as an asset in helping others.

I pray that this second edition will continue to be a great 'Godsend' to many new readers.

Michael Bentley
England
March 2005

PREFACE

This book is intended to stimulate discussion of conversion, to encourage preaching for conversion and assurance of salvation, to be a useful as a tool for mission and evangelism, to promote revival and to recover a sense of the mystery of conversion.

In this manuscript, the male pronouns and possessive forms ('he', 'his' and 'him') are used to refer *inclusively* to all humans without regard to gender. I have used the male pronouns in order to avoid potentially clumsy constructions such as 'him/her' that may impede the reader. This choice conforms to the rules of standard written English.

I must take this opportunity to express my thanks to the membership of Miller Avenue Baptist Church. This book is the fruit of one small church.

I want to thank my wife Lisa and our twin daughters,

Laura and Jenna, for lovingly supporting me during the writing of this manuscript, which required many long hours away from them. I want to also acknowledge my three older children, Dawn (Dory), Grace and Vernon, who all know Jesus as Saviour and have encouraged me on this project.

Tom Jerrells worked with me day in and day out in editing the first edition of this book. We wrestled with every concept and every sentence. In addition, a number of people in the church read various versions of the manuscript and offered me insights and challenges — Maggie Bates, Bob Burns, Katie Coddaire, Brad Friedlander, Michael Graham and Christina Rose. Thanks to each one of these special people, co-labourers of mine.

Kent Philpott
Mill Valley, California
January 1998 and June 2005

INTRODUCTION

Ten years ago my attention was drawn to the subject of conversion. For twenty-nine years of ministry I had assumed — without really thinking about it — that a person could choose to become a Christian. I assumed that he or she, by an act of the will, could decide to repent and trust in Jesus as Saviour and Lord. I had learned this standard evangelical model early on and I never questioned it.

If I had been pressed to say if I really believed a person had the power to become a Christian by means of a choice or a decision, I would probably have said no.

Not many evangelicals believe a person can literally *decide* to become a Christian, because that idea is generally understood to be inconsistent with biblical theology. Without depreciating the role of free will, is deciding to believe in Jesus Christ the same as conversion? Certainly, we understand that we are to repent and believe (see Acts 20:21), but we rightly understand that God makes both of these things possible by convicting us of our sin and revealing Jesus as Saviour to us. Indeed, most evangelicals (and I am one) speak of 'saving grace' and know that the new birth comes only through the work of the Holy Spirit. This was also true of me, but my practical evangelistic methods were not consistent with my theology.

Conversion is something God does to or for us — he births us. From our perspective, it may seem as though we have made a choice but it is actually, and completely, the work of God. For salvation to be seen as no more than a human act or choice is to misunderstand, and misrepresent, saving grace.

A STARTLING DISCOVERY

In 1994, I began to read the history of the Great Awakenings in America. What captured my attention and stopped me dead in my tracks was the controversy between Asahel Nettleton and Charles Finney in the 1820s over 'means'. Finney had introduced means or procedures, techniques or devices, by which a person could become a Christian. These included 'the altar call' or invitation and the 'sinner's prayer' which many evangelicals today depend on to 'lead a person to Christ'. Nettleton thought these techniques were contrary to biblical practice — that being, to present the gospel of Christ and depend upon the Holy Spirit to bring about conversion. Nettleton contended that the 'means' Finney employed would result in false professions of conversion.

I found myself agreeing with Nettleton — unbiblical evangelistic methodology *could* result in people thinking they had become Christians when in fact they had not. Certainly, during the many years of my ministry, some people who claimed to be Christians later proved not to be so. I was aware of this but I did not seriously consider what it meant.

Were there people in the pews — not really Christians but thinking they were Christians — who were merely fooled into thinking they were on their way to heaven?

The idea that there could be false conversion was revolutionary to me and I wondered why I had never come across it before. It was also not an easy pill to swallow because it called into question three decades of my own ministry. Armed with new information, I was compelled to rethink the true nature of Christian conversion. The result was the book *Are you really born again?* which Evangelical Press published in 1998.

A MAJOR SHIFT IN DIRECTION

Converted in 1963 through the ministry of Robert D. Lewis at the First Baptist Church of Fairfield, California, I became, *de facto*, an evangelical in the Arminian tradition. By Arminian, I mean non-Calvinistic. At the time, however, I did not know anything about Calvinism or reformed theology. (The term 'reformed' theology is broadly used to denote Calvinistic theology. I want to make it clear that I am not trying to turn people into 'Calvinists'. My focus is on the nature of conversion — a major concern for all Christians, Arminian or reformed.) The church in Fairfield practiced the kind of evangelism that Nettleton had argued against in his controversy with Finney and I, quite naturally, embraced it. Later, from 1968 to 1980, I was what might be called a charismatic evangelical in the Arminian tradition. After 1980 I was not active in charismatic ministry but I did continue to hold to a general evangelical, Arminian theology. It was not until 1997 that I began moving towards a reformed viewpoint. This brief history of my Christian life is only meant to point out that I was thoroughly steeped in the mainstream of evangelical, Arminian theology.

False conversions were more abundant in the charismatic period of my ministry than before or since. I think this is because I was more focused on charismatic expression, especially speaking in tongues, and assumed that speaking in tongues was proof of a genuine conversion. I have come to believe that this is erroneous although I am not a complete cessationist (e.g. believing that the expression of charismatic gifts of the Holy Spirit ceased with the publication of the New Testament).

There will likely always be some people who make false professions of conversion, despite our best efforts, but I see fewer people experiencing this in non-charismatic settings. Providing a 'means' or technique for someone to become a Christian or accepting some show of spirituality as a sign of conversion is no longer acceptable to me and is inconsistent with how I now view biblical conversion. After all, a means can be followed without any change in the heart and signs can be mimicked through observing others.

Suspecting that employing the usual evangelical methods to bring people to Christ *could* lead to false conversion, I started to change the way in which I conducted my ministry. It was a genuine struggle for me to come to the end of a strong evangelistic sermon and not invite people to come forward, to raise their hands or do something visible to indicate that they wanted to accept Jesus as their own personal Saviour. I gradually stopped using the standard invitation, but I never stopped urging people to repent of their sin and trust in Jesus as their Saviour and Lord. What I stopped doing was manipulating people at the end of my sermons to do what I wanted them to do — come forward and pray a prayer. As a result, I did receive some criticism from church members. I respected and considered these criticisms but I realized I had to start depending on the Holy Spirit to bring both the conviction of sin and the revelation of Jesus as Saviour and Lord.

One suggestion I examined with considerable attention was that I ought to 'cast a wide net', meaning that I should use any and all evangelistic strategies to bring as many people into the church as possible, and let God sort it out.

I should employ the latest styles of worship, entice people to make decisions, make Christianity as attractive as possible, conduct ministries that would enhance peoples lives, and so on. 'So what ', the argument went, 'if people were not genuinely converted. As long as they were in the pews, they would hear the gospel and might eventually be converted. Better that than no exposure to any form of Christianity.'

I was almost persuaded by this reasoning. After all, I am not the judge and jury; God is sovereign and he will use whatever means he wants. I had, in fact, used many techniques over the years that seemed to be successful in urging people to make a Christian commitment. But now I saw the great danger of false conversion and I wanted to trust God to do the work and not use unbiblical methods to get people converted.

REMOVING THE OFFENSE OF THE GOSPEL

The temptation in evangelism is to avoid the offense of the cross. To proclaim that there is *nothing* we can do to earn forgiveness is offensive. We want to be in control and we are revolted by the idea that God alone calls, elects and saves.

If Paul had not preached that salvation could be had in Christ alone but had taught that salvation could be achieved by obeying the Law of Moses, he would not have run into trouble with those who said otherwise. He wrote to the churches of Galatia: 'Brothers, if I am still preaching circumcision, why am I still being persecuted? In that case the offense of the cross has been abolished' (Gal. 5:11). To present Jesus' sacrifice on the cross as the only means of salvation is modified sharply by demanding circumcision as well. If we are given something to do in order to have eternal life, it dramatically changes the reality of salvation by grace *alone*. If given something to do, many will do what-ever is being asked — whether it be circumcision, baptism, saying a prayer, joining a church, changing behaviour or giving intellectual ascent to various points of doctrine.

These are things we can *do*. But it is not the same as looking to Jesus *alone* as Saviour. And precisely what I had been doing was unwittingly giving people something 'holy' and 'Christian' to do. They would generally 'do it' and conclude they had met the requirements for salvation.

WAS I RIGHT AND COULD I BE SURE?

For a few years, there was little visible evidence that I was on the right track. However, my preaching became more focused on the gospel, lifting up Jesus and the cross as strongly and clearly as I could and trusting that the Holy Spirit would bring conversion. I preached sovereign grace and the need for men and women to seek and turn to Christ as their Saviour and Lord. But without being able to count numbers of people raising their hands or somehow responding to an invitation to believe in Jesus, I had a difficult time evaluating the effectiveness of my ministry. From time to time I would question myself, revert to my old pattern and close a sermon with an 'invitation'. When I did do this, there were usually some responses — often from the same people who had responded in the past! There were also responses from people who never developed into anything like what I would expect a disciple of Jesus to be. I persisted then, preaching clear gospel messages, ending sermons with a prayer or a hymn and trusting that God would empower his Word.

You may have noticed in a previous paragraph something that might appear to be a contradiction. I said that I preached sovereign grace (or election) but that I also preached that a person must repent of their sin and trust in Jesus as Saviour and Lord. Yes, this *appears* to be a contradiction but I hold to both at once, just as C. H. Spurgeon did back in the late nineteenth century. Spurgeon was attacked by 'hyper-Calvinists' for preaching the necessity for repentance and faith and at the same time Arminians attacked him for preaching sovereign election! Spurgeon said he preached *both* because the Bible taught both. I now hold to that understanding as well. I do not offer 'works' a person can follow to achieve salvation. Rather, the Holy Spirit must do the *whole* work, from repentance to faith. [I recommend Iain H. Murray's *Spurgeon v. Hyper-Calvinism* (The Banner of Truth Trust, 1996) for more on this crucial point.]

Slowly, encouraging results began to be seen in my ministry. One here, another there — people were converted while they were in church, at home, in the car, or at work. As they discovered their new birth, they began to confess their faith in Jesus in varying ways, some by direct personal statement, others by baptism and others by simply living out what it is to love Jesus and his Word. It was wonderful to see God at work!

CONVERSION IS ALWAYS A MYSTERY

Conversion is still a mystery to me and I am sure it always will be. However, the possibility that false conversions were common in evangelical circles seemed probable to me and prompted me to write this book back in 1998. Based on responses I have received as a result (letters, phone calls, and emails from all over the world — mostly from Christian leaders in the Arminian tradition), I now consider the issue of false conversion to be more serious than I had first imagined (see Appendix III).

Here are some typical emails: 'Now I understand why so many drifted away and never became disciples', or 'It never occurred to me that [name of person] was not actually a believer. I expected a real Christian to have a minimal interest in things Christian, but there was nothing.' 'I knew something was amiss but I never guessed it was something so serious as a false conversion.' 'A few times people suggested I was not really a Christian but I didn't believe them.' Most often, I would read something like: 'I wondered what was wrong, but everyone continually assured me I was a Christian.' Occasionally a correspondent would report his or her own conversion, which came, to that individual, as quite a surprise.

This book has caused difficulties for some people. It is unsettling to bring up the subject of false conversion. Several pastors who came to agree with my position ran into problems with their congregations. One Lutheran minister was forced to leave his church when a largely unconverted membership grew tired of him preaching 'law and gospel'. However, a few were converted and my friend felt that he had done the right thing in spite of the rejection. Another pastor, from an independent Bible church in Singapore, saw his congregation dwindle to the point that he grew discouraged and resigned. I received other similar reports. To a pastor whose church I knew well, I said that if I preached a few sermons in his church, he might find that a significant number in his congregation would discover they were unconverted. He quickly responded, 'You are *not* preaching in my church.'

And this is what it comes down to: What are we really doing? Are we simply filling the pews or do we actually care whether our family members, our friends and members of our congregations hear Jesus say, 'Well done, good and faithful servant... Enter into the joy of your lord' (Matt. 25:21, NKJV). Would we rather they hear him say, 'I never knew you; depart from me' (Matt. 7:23, NKJV)? How difficult it is to have eternity in our minds! We easily focus on just the here and now.

Reader, the stakes are high. One passage that grips me and gives me courage to act upon my convictions is 2 Corinthians 2:15–16:

For we are to God the aroma of Christ among those who are being saved and those who are perishing. To the one we are the smell of death; to the other the fragrance of life. Who is equal to such a task?

A MATTER OF LIFE AND DEATH

In preaching for conversion, I would rather risk personal rejection and ridicule than provide a quick and easy method of using human means to acquire questionable professions of conversion. In my mind, it is a 'win-win' thing to question our own conversion and that of others. On the one hand, we may see that we are converted and thus have greater assurance of our salvation. On the other, we may see that we are not converted and then seek Jesus for salvation. The great danger is in not realizing that a profession of conversion is false — then there is no hope at all. As the apostle contended, it is a matter of eternal life and death.

Preaching the gospel of Christ and his cross will cause trouble and many pastors and preachers will not do anything that has the potential to drive people away. It is a wrong priority, for sure, but I understand the feeling. Many pastors feel pressured by their denomination, association, church council or board of elders to keep in place the standard evangelistic practices and so record conversions. More than that, it is an excruciating emotional experience to see people leave the church. It is enough to drive preachers to discouragement and depression — I can personally attest to this. I was accused of becoming non-evangelistic when I started to trust the Holy Spirit to bring conversion rather than relying on various techniques. This pressure is often enough to keep faulty methods in place in a person's ministry.

Christians may find it unpleasant to question the eternal destiny of those close to them. We tend to avoid talking about things that might create conflict. For myself, I have gradually found the courage to speak the gospel message and learned to help a person examine whether there is anything approximating a genuine conversion in their life. This potentially awkward situation is preferred to being silent about the truly central reality of life — whether someone is truly converted or not.

I am hopeful that the tide is turning and many Christians are seeing what their real work is and are going about it. My prayer is that this second edition is sharper, clearer and stronger and will be useful to those who seek to share the grace and mercy of God our Saviour with others.

1

CHRISTIANIZATION OR CONVERSION?

John said he still believed in Jesus. He told me he became a Christian at a church camp when he was twelve. He was baptized and began attending church services at least twice a week. In his college years he 'slacked off' but after he got married he and his wife regularly attended church together. Everything appeared to be in place spiritually; he had even considered the possibility of going into the ministry. He had few doubts and lived a clean life. His performance appeared to indicate he was an exemplary Christian. However, one day he got tired of it and 'quit' being a Christian. He did not take up another religion — he simply dropped out. When we met later at a memorial service, John told me he felt better now that he was away from the church even though he knew his wife and family were praying for him. John had conformed to standards of

Christian belief and behaviour but he had never understood that he was guilty before God because of his sin and
so he felt no need to trust in Jesus as his Saviour. He
thought highly of Jesus as a great spiritual teacher, but he
was not converted.

José, from San Jose, glared at me from behind the bars of
his San Quentin prison cell. He did not want a Bible from
me. He had been given one while he was at the San
Francisco County Jail. José had been raised in the Roman
Catholic Church but he claimed to have been 'baptized in
the Spirit' as a teenager at a big church in Los Angeles. At
the age of thirty-five he was serving a 'three strikes' sentence
(in California, any third conviction for a serious offender
means a mandatory sentence of twenty-five years to life)
and wondered what had happened to his Christianity.
After talking with José for an hour or so, I realized what his
problem was: he had no idea *why* Jesus died on the cross,
and he had no sense of forgiveness. Moreover, he did not pray
or read his Bible, he refused to attend the worship services
at the chapel and he looked down on those convicts who
claimed to be Christians — yet he claimed to have received
'the baptism of the Spirit'. José had been 'Christianized'; he
had been tricked.

Right next to José's cell was that of Mike from Oakland.
Younger than José by a dozen years, he had been in lock-
ups for twelve years and had just 'graduated' to San Quentin.
Raised in a Baptist church, he had been immersed in the
baptismal tank at the age of five, sang in the choir from
the age of six and began preaching when he was nine. At
seventeen he was in the California Youth Authority. At the
age of twenty-five he converted to the Nation of Islam. I
asked Mike: 'Were you really a Christian in the first place?'
He said, 'Come on, man, don't talk like that! I just told you
all I did in church.' Mike had no conversion experience
though — that is, he neither expressed a sense of needing
to be forgiven nor of needing a Saviour. The way he put it

was that he always believed. Mike, my conviction was, had been very heavily Christianized and when that wore off he was open for something else to take its place.

I met Sherie when she attended a divorce recovery workshop I hosted. Her second marriage had failed and a friend had suggested she come to the workshop. During the course of the workshop I spent several hours talking with her. After the failure of her first marriage, some friends came to her rescue and helped her put the pieces of her life back together; she accompanied them to their church. She said she had been a committed Christian from the moment she was 'saved'. She had even led worship in a charismatic church and had been involved in ministry at a local jail. Several years later she met a non-Christian, fell in love, married and abruptly left the church and her Christianity behind, shocking and disappointing her Christian friends. She was very aware, however, of what had happened to her — she simply embraced the lifestyle and philosophy of her rescuers. She thought she was Christian because she did all the right things, said the right things and strongly 'believed'. But, she gradually lost interest and her new marriage gave her an excuse to leave the church.

Bob, whom I met while officiating at a wedding, was a typical middle-class, church-going American. He told me, and I summarize: 'I'm a baptized member of a Christ-centered church and I've prayed to receive Jesus many times and I've rededicated my life many times. I've been through discipleship classes, I've submitted to the lordship of Christ and you could say my life is in order. But why don't I feel like a Christian? Why don't I believe like a Christian? Why don't I enjoy being a Christian?'

Gladys made a decision to become a follower of Jesus in 1975. She became convinced that Jesus rose from the dead and would return to take her to heaven. As a student at a liberal arts college, she embraced an evolutionary theory that suggested there was no need for God and that men invented religion in order to make sense of life and bring order to society. After a failed romance, she began studying eastern religions. She soon tired of that and took up reading the Bible and other Christian literature. She was looking for proofs that God was real and after exploring Christian apologetic material, Gladys became convinced that Christianity was true. The Christian world-view, Gladys realized, was credible. Many intelligent people were Christians and the cultures spawned by Christianity were the most substantial in the world. Christian art, history, music, architecture and Christian rites and ceremonies were all viable and compelling to her. Also, at about the same time, she had found a church that provided a sense of belonging and community. Wanting to identify with her new friends on a deeper level, she openly declared that she had decided to believe in Jesus. Later, in 1980, she alternately attended two of America's major Christian-based cults, being unable to make up her mind which was the true religion. In 1990 she packed up her religious books and took them to a charity; that was the year she decided she wasn't a Christian after all.

During the thirty years of my ministry, I have spoken with many people like John, José, Mike, Sherie, Bob and Gladys. Often raised in the church, these people usually participated in the normal activities of a church, including baptism, membership classes, public statements of faith and discipleship classes. Yet some did not continue as Christians and others had no inner conviction they were Christians. Why? Because they were never converted in the first place!

THE DANGERS OF CHRISTIANIZATION

Many people think they are born-again Christians when in fact they have merely been Christianized. To be infused with Christian principles, to participate in the normal activities of a church, is never the same as experiencing actual conversion. The false conversion that comes with Christianization may eventually cause people to look for something else to satisfy their spiritual hunger. Most often, however, people assume their Christianization is true conversion.

It may be thought that I have too high a view of conversion — meaning that I expect too much of a person who says he is a Christian. The argument is this: If a person is not an adherent of another religion or philosophy and is a good person who believes in God, Jesus, the Bible, attends church once in a while, and so on, isn't that enough? I admit that many inside and outside Christian circles would say that it is enough. But when we look at what it means to be a Christian in the Scriptures, it is apparent that it is *not* enough. True Christianity generally begins with a conviction that sin has separated us from God and that Jesus Christ is Saviour and Lord. Once God opens our eyes to this reality, we receive the new birth in a way and manner we do not control. The lifelong experience of growing up into the fulness of Jesus begins there. And although the believer is not perfect, there will still be *some* evidence of their new birth right from the beginning. This was certainly evident in those who were converted in Scripture — people like Matthew, Zacchaeus, Paul and many others. There is life following a new birth; there is nothing when there is a stillbirth.

While growing up, I too was Christianized and did not understand the true message of the gospel. An illustration of this took place when I was applying for the air force. A section of the paperwork I had to fill out had to do with religious affiliation. I ticked the box marked 'Christian' and for denomination I put 'Episcopalian'. As far as I understood, I was Christian. Since I was not Jewish, Hindu, Buddhist, Muslim, etc., I thought that I must be a Christian. I had never been in an Episcopalian church and I had no clue as to what an Episcopalian was. I had, however, read Vance

Packard's book *The Status Seekers* and I had learned that the Episcopalian denomination was the most prestigious. Being a status-seeker myself, I became an 'Episcopalian Christian' by ticking a box.

I am not alone. In the USA we are born into a so-called 'Christian culture'. I and my contemporaries grew up learning something about church, God and the Bible — by osmosis at least. Many of us were baptized, became members of a church and even attended Sunday school, especially when we were young. It only made sense that we were Christians. This is not so prevalent today because many young people have little or no idea about church and Christianity. Perhaps it is clearer for young people now — they do not presume they are 'Christian'. But it was not that way for me.

It is a common understanding among Christians that conversion occurs as a result of such things as coming forward in a church service and praying 'the sinner's prayer', being baptized, joining a church, reciting a statement of faith, making a decision to believe in Jesus or behaving like a Christian. In themselves, these things tend to Christianize rather than convert, and relying on them as proofs of conversion lacks any biblical authority. There are the exceptions of course — God will do what he will do. He will convert people through all sorts of ways, but in our evangelism and preaching we must put into practice sound biblical methodology rather than relying on tradition and 'what seems to work'.

The story of the Rev. William Haslam, an Anglican priest in the mid-eighteenth century in Cornwall, England, vividly illustrates this idea of Christianization. Born into the church, he was baptized, confirmed and ordained. He met every requirement of the church — without being converted. His congregation in Cornwall knew that he was unconverted and they began to pray for him. One day while preaching in his own church, he was converted.*

Those events took place long ago, but the same story is repeated in our own day. Why are so many people merely Christianized rather than converted? Why do so many people experience the form and not the substance? The answer lies in the fact that true biblical conversion is a mystery that men and women will never fully comprehend. Biblical conversion is accomplished by God alone; salvation belongs totally to God. We, however, are not content with this and so have invented means by which a person is supposed to be able to receive salvation. When people fulfill whatever is proffered as means of salvation, they are pronounced Christians. Men and women, by nature, seek acceptance and approval; most do not have a sense that salvation and the forgiveness of sin is the real issue. From a desire to belong, people will often do certain things, almost mindlessly, and what is actually taking place is that they are becoming Christianized or falsely converted.

REACHING OUT TO THE CHRISTIANIZED

Christianization poses an exceptional problem for preachers because people have been taught to rely on the prescribed recitations and rites of their churches for salvation rather than coming to Jesus for forgiveness and salvation. The preacher must challenge the façade of Christianization with conversion-oriented preaching.

It must be said that the unconverted do not like such preaching! They will often vigorously oppose what is in fact their only hope. In response to conversion-oriented preaching they may become angry, sometimes to the point of violence. They can only take so much preaching for conversion before they either go off looking for a 'friendly' church that has a minister who delivers 'positive messages'

---

* Evangelical Press and Earthen Vessel Publishing have jointly republished the account of Rev. Haslam's conversion. *From death into life* is the title of Haslam's account of his conversion and the amazing events that followed.

or, worse still, they attempt to stifle a conversion-oriented preacher by political maneuvering within the church. People who have been simply Christianized and not truly converted can become dangerous within a congregation. They can split churches, cause acrimonious dissension and sometimes end the ministry of a conversion-oriented pastor.

It is not a pleasant task to awaken the 'righteous'. The 'righteous' do not respond to Jesus, but sinners will. Jesus found that to be so. Self-righteous Pharisees attacked Jesus and he responded, 'I have not come to call the righteous, but sinners to repentance' (Luke 5:32).

Christianization is a powerful delusion. It results in people erroneously thinking that they are safely on their way to heaven. These lost 'righteous' are, in the words of the Puritan preacher Jonathan Dickinson, 'sleeping on the brink of hell'. The gospel preacher must wake them up! What is the alternative? Surely one day the unconverted will hear Jesus say, 'I never knew you. Away from me, you evildoers!' (Matt. 7:23).

2

THE MYSTERY OF CONVERSION

Hank Hanegraaff, known as the 'Bible Answer Man', wrote the following prayer in the Christian Research Institute's newsletter:

> *Simply bow your head right now and pray:*
> *Heavenly Father,*
> *I thank you that you have provided a way for me to have a relationship with you. I realize I am a sinner. I thank you that you are my perfect Father. I ask you, Jesus, to be my Saviour and Lord. I repent and receive your perfection in exchange for my sin; in Jesus' name I pray. Amen.†*

---

† Christian Research Institute's Newsletter, Winter/Spring 1996, vol. 9, issue 1.

I heartily endorse the theology expressed in this prayer — especially what it says about Jesus and his perfect provision for us. However, is Hanegraaff correct when he goes on to say, 'If you have prayed this prayer, you can know with certainty that you have eternal life...'?

In 1963, I prayed a 'sinner's prayer' with a deacon from the Baptist church I attended, but I was not converted until six months later. My father, Vernon Philpott, did not 'go forward' at the invitation during a Billy Graham Crusade but was converted later that night while lying in his bed.

For thirty years I have prayed with many people who were seeking salvation. I have almost always relied on some version of the familiar sinner's prayer. Some were converted and some were not converted — or so it seemed to me as I looked for signs that would indicate whether they were born again or not. (I will describe these signs in chapter 6.)

God will do what he will do and the sinner's prayer may be used by God to bring about conversion. Billy Graham, who has long been a hero of the faith for me, popularized the sinner's prayer. I do not want to demean his ministry but, at the same time, I think that salvation is not assured by merely saying that prayer. In fact, the act of reciting the sinner's prayer may give false assurance to certain people who are not genuinely converted. After all, praying a prayer is a 'work', a conscious act, and no one is born again by an act of the will. Over the course of my ministry, I have met many people who were not born again despite their many prayers for salvation.

CONVERSION INVOLVES A PARADOX

Conversion is a mystery. Conversion is not guaranteed by saying a simple prayer or, for that matter, a complex, and theologically correct one. Conversion, or the new birth, involves a paradox — that is, two thoughts that seem at odds with each other and appear impossible for us to harmonize. For instance, conversion is a work of God, yet we are called to 'turn to God in repentance and have faith in our Lord Jesus' (Acts 20:21). So then, *God works and we repent and believe* — this is a paradox or a mystery. To admit that a mystery exists is neither a compromise nor a concession; rather, it is a necessary admission in light of the biblical testimony and our desire to be faithful to what Scripture has revealed about the nature of conversion.

The central problem is that this mystery has so often been swept aside by the invention of purely human means to receive salvation. The result of ignoring the mystery is Christianization, or false conversion.

One problem in using the sinner's prayer is illustrated through my voluntary work at San Quentin State Prison. Most of the time I go from cell to cell and talk to the convicts. Many of them report that they are born-again Christians. Thanks be to God, there is hardly a prison, county jail or institution for juvenile offenders that does not have concerned Christians undertaking evangelistic work. As a result, many incarcerated persons have heard the wonderful gospel of our Lord Jesus and have prayed for salvation. Some have prayed those prayers many times, in many places, and they testify that they are converted. Yet, after years and years, the spiritual life of many 'converted' convicts is a flat line. There are no signs of life! When the 'born-again' person manifests no desire to pray, no interest in the Scriptures, no desire for worship and praise, no love for Jesus and his cross — is there any *life* in that person?

'Are you a Christian?' A person may reply, 'Well, I prayed to receive Jesus.' Is this adequate? Where is the acknowledgement of being lost and the futility of self-righteousness? Where is the cross of Jesus and his cleansing blood? Where is the affirmation that Jesus is the living Lord and Messiah? Where is that coming to Jesus for forgiveness and salvation?

As a pastor, I am often dismayed by the testimonies of 'conversion' that I hear. People believe they are converted by baptism, by receiving communion, by being good and loving, by not hurting anyone, by being a member of a church or by having 'gone forward' to pray the sinner's prayer. Can I be assured that a person with a 'weak', unbiblical and confused conversion testimony has his name recorded in the Lamb's book of life?

Recently I imagined one of my church members standing before God's terrible throne of judgement and hearing Jesus say, 'I never knew you. Away from me, you evildoers!' (Matt. 7:23). And then that person replied, 'But that preacher, that pastor of mine, he never told me of my danger; he never warned me of my true condition. So I never came to an assurance of salvation, and now it is too late.' I was stunned to think that people in my own congregation might not be converted.

I cannot determine with certainty whether a person is truly born again. I have no spiritual gift that allows such insight; I claim no special anointing or knowledge. Yet I can often see whether or not the life of Jesus is in a person. There are signs of being a Christian, even in the 'babe in Christ'. If there is a love for God, love for the Saviour, interest in the Bible, concern for worship, praise and prayer, then I believe a biblical conversion has probably taken place. (Many of the great American preachers of the eighteenth century would have said in such a case that a person was 'hopefully' converted.) However, people who say they are born again but show no signs of conversion are probably not converted. The most dangerous situation of all is that a person imagines himself to be converted when in fact he is not. Christianization, or false conversion, is a sure road to hell.

Consider the case of a man who for many years confesses faith in Christ and is active in a church (perhaps in a leadership position), but then abandons his faith, rejects the church and joins another religion. In my ministry, I have seen such people embrace religions like Islam and Buddhism. This is more common than I like to think. Were such people converted in the first place? After a period, will they come back to Christ? After observing such people and questioning them as to reason and motive, I have found in every instance that there was no true conversion present in the beginning. Instead of true conversion I found Christianization — a person went along with his childhood teachings, identified with the beliefs of his parents, conformed to church practices in order to accepted by Christian friends and leaders, and so on. (My conclusion may seem self-serving and unverifiable. If so, you might put it to the test when circumstances make it possible.)

This description illustrates something that has been observed all the way back to the early church. The Apostle John was aware of people in the church of his day who were not Christians. Probably in reference to those who went on to embrace Gnosticism, he wrote, 'They went out from us, but they did not really belong to us. For if they had belonged to us, they would have remained with us; but their going showed that none of them belonged to us' (1 John 2:19). Most pastors understand this verse. They have known people — good people, spiritual people, zealous people, loving people — who claimed to be Christians, but were not. Some of them will leave a church if there is clear, consistent preaching of the cross (or be converted!), but where the gospel is not faithfully proclaimed, these same people will mistakenly think they are included in the kingdom of God.

A WORK OF GOD

Conversion is the result of the sovereign work of God in Christ. God's Holy Spirit gives a person the gift of repentance and faith so that they can turn from their sin and believe in Jesus. Salvation is all of God. The *way* an individual is converted, from a human point of view, is a mystery. However, all are urged — even commanded — to 'believe in the Lord Jesus' (Acts 16:31).

In the Bible no particular *method* is given about how a person is to believe. Even when the Philippian jailer asked

Paul and Silas what he must do to be saved, the response was only: 'Believe in the Lord Jesus, and you will be saved...' (Acts 16:31). Although they had given him nothing to do or say, we find later on in the story that he did in fact believe — but we do not read of any steps that he took to get there.

In the prologue to John's Gospel we find the well-known sentence: 'Yet to all who received him, to those who believed in his name, he gave the right to become children of God — children born not of natural descent, nor of human decision or a husband's will, but born of God' (John 1:12–13). How do we believe in Jesus? How do we 'receive' him? John does not say — but we would like him to have done so. In the face of the Bible's silence on this crucial issue, many have unhappily, and dangerously, given answers. But no answer can be biblically correct since the Bible does not explicitly tell us *how* a person is born again, except to say it is not of our own will or doing. (In Ephesians 2:8–9 Paul makes it clear that even faith is a gift of God.)

Many readers will undoubtedly have seen photographs of Michelangelo's painting, *The Creation*, on the ceiling of the Sistine Chapel in Rome. The painting is that of the Creator, God Almighty, reaching down to man, his fallen and beloved creature. Adam is shown reaching up but not touching the finger of God. For me, this space between God and man (which is only a few inches in the painting) symbolizes the mystery of conversion. It is as though we want to close the gap and bring God and man together; we want to rearrange the painting; we want to resolve the mystery — a tantalizing temptation. We want to be able to offer concrete and do-it-yourself methods for achieving salvation. And in so doing, we have taken (as if we could!) salvation right out of the hand of God. Despite all our attempts to invent methods that make conversion seem obvious and visible to us, these merely serve to Christianize people without truly converting them. Conversion is, and will remain, a mystery.

3

TRUE CONVERSION

No subject is more important to consider than conversion because we will all die, sooner or later, and then we will face judgement.

CONVERSION BEGINS WITH GOD

Conversion comes after some kind of presentation of the message of the gospel of Jesus Christ is made. This presentation could be through the spoken word (such as preaching), or through television, film, drama, music, tract, audiotape, video, book, Bible, etc. Somehow the message of the gospel comes to a person. He may be seeking the kingdom of God; he may be simply curious; or he may just be at the right place at the right time. He may be tormented and grief-stricken, or be joyful and self-satisfied. Nevertheless, the message of the gospel comes to the person's attention. Paul wrote: 'Faith comes from hearing the message, and the message is heard through the word of Christ' (Rom. 10:17).

When I heard Robert D. Lewis preach about Jesus at the First Baptist Church in Fairfield, California, I knew nothing of the gospel. Worse, what I thought I knew was inaccurate. Nothing Christian made sense to me — not the Bible, not the words of hymns, and especially not the preaching. However, one truth eventually got through to me: *I was a sinner who was far away from God.* It made me both angry and sad — I was convinced I was lost! The realization that I was lost came from God's Holy Spirit because it is the Holy Spirit who convicts us of sin (John 16:8). This was not an idea I would naturally (or easily) embrace about myself. The fact is I was quite confident as a young man and not anxious or full of guilt.

The unconverted are not usually troubled about their sin. Rather sin may be unnoticed, excused, redefined and/or defended. It must be so, for who would easily own up to it? The unconverted person may recognize his destructive behaviour towards himself or others, but he is unlikely to think of his sin as a violation of God's law and an offence to a holy and righteous Judge unless the Holy Spirit shows that to him.

The second truth the Holy Spirit revealed to me was that *Jesus is the Saviour.*

In both instances (the revelation that I was lost and the revelation that Jesus is the Saviour) nothing spectacular happened. There was no voice from heaven; there were no observable phenomena of any kind. Nor were there any unusual or overwhelming feelings. There may indeed be feelings and emotions involved, but generally the convicting work of the Spirit is thoughtful, imaginative and spiritual — a conflict of wills. Spiritual conviction is stronger than anything external could be; it is inescapable, compelling and gripping.

For the first time in my life I saw my need and at the same time my attention was riveted on Jesus. I cannot explain how this happened I only know it did. My conversion followed what might be called a classical conversion pattern and I have witnessed the same in many other people. One thing is clear: I did not figure anything out about Jesus on my own. Jesus said, 'No one can come to me unless the Father who sent me draws him' (John 6:44; see also Matt. 16:17; John 16:14–15; Acts 16:14; Gal. 1:15–16). I was drawn to Jesus, but I did not understand it at all.

The Holy Spirit reveals to us both our own lost condition and that Jesus is the Saviour. The following are biblical references that support these truths. Paul wrote, 'For the message of the cross is foolishness to those who are perishing, but to us who are being saved it is the power of God' (1 Cor. 1:18). Paul went on to say, 'The man without the Spirit does not accept the things that come from the Spirit of God, for they are foolishness to him, and he cannot understand them, because they are spiritually discerned' (1 Cor. 2:14).

Not only are we unable (due to our fallen condition) to know the truth of the gospel but we are also under the influence of the enemy, the devil. Paul writes: 'The god of this age has blinded the minds of unbelievers, so that they cannot see the light of the gospel of the glory of Christ, who is the image of God' (2 Cor. 4:4). The unconverted person faces a hopeless situation given the forces that are marshalled against him. Although he may be acquainted with religious philosophies and theologies, he is blind to the message of the gospel of Jesus Christ.

A key passage on conversion is found in John 3. Jesus told Nicodemus, an esteemed religious leader, that 'no one can see the kingdom of God unless he is born again' (John 3:3). This made no sense to Nicodemus. How could a grown man be reborn? Jesus did not explain how. He said that rebirth is beyond human control: 'The wind blows wherever it pleases. You hear its sound, but you cannot tell where it comes from or where it is going. So it is with everyone born of the Spirit' (John 3:8). Nicodemus practiced his religion very carefully and with great reward from his peers. He did everything he thought was required of him. However, he could not, by his own volition, cause himself to be born again; he could not give spiritual birth to himself. Only God, the Father, gives new birth.

After the Holy Spirit of God has convicted us of our sin and revealed Jesus to us as the one who saves us from sin and its terrible penalty, we must come to Jesus for cleansing from sin; we must come to Jesus *exclusively* and trust him for forgiveness. We must come to the risen Saviour, who shed his blood for us on the cross, and throw ourselves upon God's mercy. Out of the Father's great love for us, he sent his unique, eternal Son to this earth. God the Son became flesh, became a man, and lived among us. God the Father sent his Son to die on the cross in fulfilment of the prophecies of Scripture, and placed upon him all our sin. Jesus was the perfect sacrifice because he was holy and pure and without sin.

HOW DOES AN UNCONVERTED PERSON COME TO JESUS?

I do not want to suggest a 'method' for conversion but since Jesus is the living, resurrected Lord, we *can* have a relationship with him. We can come to Jesus in prayer, confessing and repenting of our sin. We can come to Jesus for his mercy. We can come to Jesus to have our sin covered by his blood. We can come to Jesus. We can talk to Jesus. We can ask Jesus to save us. We can come to Jesus through prayer — not a special prayer, not through a particular set of words that can be written down or recited — just through talking to Jesus about what is on our heart.

Jesus died in the place of sinners; the blood of Jesus cleanses us from all our sins, however awful they may be. biblical faith, which is trust in Jesus alone, is not derived from any work or action that we can do. Faith means trusting and relying exclusively on Jesus and what he accomplished on the cross. But saving faith is impossible without the enabling work of the Holy Spirit. In Acts 13:48 it is written that 'all who were appointed for eternal life believed'. To believe in Jesus is to come to him for salvation. Faith is not an idea, notion, wish, hope, doctrine or theology about Jesus. Biblical faith is trusting that only Jesus can and will save us, and we are *given* this saving faith.

Jesus declared, 'All that the Father gives me will come to me, and whoever comes to me I will never drive away' (John 6:37). Whoever comes to Jesus is given to Jesus by the Father. First, there is God's work; then, by the enabling of the Holy Spirit, a person trusts in Jesus for salvation. It is clear that no one initiates a move toward God out of his own will. No mechanism or set way is given as to how a person comes to Jesus. Instead, there is that gap that I referred to as a mystery in the previous chapter. Only God knows the mystery of how a person comes to Jesus. When someone does come to Jesus, however, he or she is converted and freely receives forgiveness of sin and everlasting life.

Over the years I have noticed that when the Scripture is silent on some point, it is for a reason. If we knew the method by which conversion occurred, we would surely attempt to control it; we would add to it; we would corrupt it. Salvation belongs to God; it is his work. Yes, a person comes to Jesus and he is wonderfully and mysteriously converted. The Holy Spirit brings a person to Jesus in a way we do not understand.

People are converted in many different ways. One person who recognized his lost condition and was seeking salvation was converted when he read about the substitutionary death of Jesus on the cross in a booklet by Charles Stanley. Another person, having been merely Christianized for many years and being entirely miserable, was converted instantly during a sermon on the living, resurrected Christ.

I know of one person who was converted while singing one of Charles Wesley's hymns.

During the First Great Awakening in America (between about 1735 and 1745) tens of thousands of people were converted without responding to any appeals to come forward or to pray a specific prayer. While John Wesley, George Whitefield, Gilbert Tennant, Jonathan Edwards and many others were actually preaching, people were being converted. There was loud groaning as people agonized over their sin; men and women fainted out of fear of having broken God's law. In the case of Gilbert Tennant, it was common for people to be converted *after* his preaching — on their way home, lying in bed that evening, the next morning at breakfast, or later in the day while out ploughing in the field. So it was in the great revivals and awakenings throughout history. So it is today.

Any person who is convicted of his sin and sees Jesus as the remedy for his sin can come, by the power of the Holy Spirit, to Jesus. Acts 16:31 is a clear declaration of the gospel: 'Believe in the Lord Jesus, and you will be saved — you and your household.' That was the answer Paul and Silas gave to the Philippian jailer's question: 'What must I do to be saved?' So, what did the jailer do? Luke does not tell us. The jailer was baptized, but the act of baptism does not save. Baptism follows conversion; it does not produce it! The fact is, there is no mechanism; there is no sinner's prayer, no coming forward, no testimony, no work at all. The jailer had heard the testimony of Paul and Silas. The Holy Spirit convinced the jailer of his desperate need and revealed Jesus to him as Saviour. That is how Jesus said it would be. The jailer was converted and we are not told how; he was simply commanded to believe in the Lord Jesus for salvation — and he did.

Instead of preaching for true conversions, many preachers have resorted to gimmicks such as church-growth techniques, 'how-to' fifteen-minute sermons and forms of 'feel-good' entertainment to get 'seekers' into the pews. Rarely do we find preaching for true conversion. One reason for this may be that many pastors have discarded the doctrine of hell and have become blind to the possibility that their parishioners may be heading there. I believe many conversion-oriented preachers resort to unbiblical methods to effect conversion, such as the sinner's prayer, because these methods have become the 'tradition' in many evangelical churches.

In the days of Solomon Stoddard's 'Halfway Covenant', people were baptized, admitted into church membership and even ordained as ministers despite the fact that they were unconverted. We face the same problem today. Therefore, we need preachers with the boldness of Jonathan Edwards (the grandson and successor to Stoddard at the First Church in Northampton, Massachusetts) to preach the necessity of true conversion. If we do not preach for true conversion, unconverted people in our churches will one day hear Jesus say, 'I never knew you. Away from me, you evildoers!'

4

CONVERSION: THE OBJECTIVE FACTS

Jesus must be at the centre of our consideration of true conversion. He must be at the centre because of who he is and what he did. The person and work of Jesus Christ are the objective aspects of conversion.

When I was converted I knew very little of Jesus; I would have failed the most elementary quiz. At that time, I was so naïve I might have believed any heretical doctrine. It is rare that an unbeliever can understand the complexities of the doctrine of salvation. Thank God, to be converted, a person does not have to be able to grasp every theological detail! If the comprehension of complicated theological concepts was required for salvation, then a doctrine would develop which emphasized salvation through knowledge (this would be an example of 'Christian' Gnosticism). Merely *knowing* correct doctrine never converted anyone.

The exposition of the message of Jesus could fill entire libraries; yet it can be delivered succinctly in just a short sermon, a personal conversation or a letter. This chapter, however, will focus on the basics of who Jesus is and what Jesus did.

WHO JESUS IS

The image of the Messiah in the Old Testament

Jesus is Immanuel, meaning 'God with us' (Isa. 7:14; Matt. 1:23). Jesus is God 'in the flesh'. To come to Jesus is the same as coming to God. Jesus is the Messiah, meaning 'Anointed One', the long-promised Deliverer. He is 'Mighty God' and 'Everlasting Father' (Isa. 9:6). Jesus is not the Father but has the same nature and will as the Father. These are clear points. However, these truths were not clear to the Jewish leaders in the first century A.D. They were expecting a Messiah who would be a military/political leader and who would miraculously deliver the Jews from the tyranny of Rome.

In the Old Testament, there are two conflicting images of the Messiah: Messiah, Son of David and, Messiah, Son of Joseph. Messiah, Son of David, suggests a great hero like King David who would rescue the people and establish a mighty and prosperous nation. Messiah, Son of Joseph, suggests the Suffering Servant of Isaiah who would, like Joseph of the many-coloured coat, save people through his suffering. We find this description of the Messiah in Isaiah 53 and Psalm 22 where it is foretold that the Messiah would die and take the sin of the people upon himself. But this Messiah would (like David) also save his people from all their enemies. Messiah, Son of Joseph, has already come; we await Messiah, Son of David. To put in another way, the first coming of Messiah was when the virgin Mary gave birth to Jesus in Bethlehem; the second will be when this same Jesus (Messiah, Son of David), now King of kings and Lord of lords, returns at the end of the age and establishes the everlasting kingdom of God.

Jesus is the perfect sacrifice and his blood must be shed to cleanse us from sin. This idea is clearly typified in the Jewish sacrificial system, which required the slaying of animals for the people's sin. Jesus is the ultimate Passover Lamb. In Egypt it was the sight of the blood on and over the doors of the Israelites' homes that saved the Israelites from death. Now, once and for all, the blood of Jesus saves men and women from death. John the Baptist, the last great prophet of Israel, said of Jesus, 'Look, the Lamb of God, who takes away the sin of the world!' (John 1:29).

The image of the Messiah in the New Testament

Jesus is the Word become flesh (John 1:14). Jesus was with God in the beginning; Jesus is the eternal Son of God. He is God, and he will always be God. Jesus did not begin his existence with his birth in Bethlehem. At birth, Jesus took on human flesh (this is known as the incarnation). Paul tells us that Jesus 'made himself nothing, taking the very nature of a servant, being made in human likeness' (Phil. 2:7). The Scripture says very little about *how* the Son of God became flesh.

Jesus is 'the image of the invisible God' (Col. 1:15). To see Jesus is to see God. The Father, the Son and the Holy Spirit are of the same substance and nature. We encounter one God as the Father/Creator, Son and Holy Spirit. Certainly we do not fully understand the doctrine of the trinity even though it is in God's revelation, the Bible. The trinity, the three in one, or the one in three, meets the criteria of Deuteronomy 6:4: 'Hear, O Israel: The Lord our God, the Lord is one.' Here God is referred to in Hebrew as *echad*, translated by the English 'one'. It means God is a unit, somewhat like a husband and wife are one unit or *echad*

(Gen. 2:24). A husband, a wife, two people, but one unit. The trinity is three, but one unit.

Philip, one of the apostles, said to Jesus, 'Lord, show us the Father and that will be enough for us.' Jesus replied, 'Don't you know me, Philip, even after I have been among you such a long time? Anyone who has seen me has seen the Father' (John 14:8–9). Jesus is not the Father; the Father is not the Son. Philip wants to know God, to know who God is. Jesus tells him that to see and know him (Jesus) is the same as to see and know God, because Jesus is God — God in the flesh.

John writes: 'The Word became flesh and made his dwelling among us. We have seen his glory, the glory of the One and Only, who came from the Father, full of grace and truth' (John 1:14). This revelation was God's eternal plan, set in place prior to the creation of the universe. Peter wrote: 'He [Jesus] was chosen before the creation of the world, but was revealed in these last times for your sake' (1 Peter 1:20).

At the right time in history, Jesus was born in Bethlehem. As Paul has written: 'But when the time had fully come, God sent his Son, born of a woman, born under law, to redeem those under law, that we might receive the full rights of sons' (Gal. 4:4–5).

The ministry of Jesus

Jesus fulfilled all the prophecies concerning the coming Messiah that are recorded in the Old Testament, including the nature, birth, ministry, life and death of the Messiah. His mother conceived him by a miracle of the Holy Spirit. The virgin Mary gave birth to him while she was in Bethlehem. He was both fully human and fully God, and he lived a sinless life, although he was tempted just like any other human. Jesus resisted the temptation to sin through his complete and utter dependence on God the Father.

Having fulfilled his family duties and having reached the age when a rabbi would commence teaching (around thirty years old), Jesus began preaching about the imminence of the kingdom of God. He gathered just twelve disciples, though many other men and women were constantly with him, and he spent three years preparing these men for his departure and for their eventual ministry.

At the end of his earthly ministry, he was arrested, unfairly tried, beaten and disfigured, humiliated and scourged. He was executed by crucifixion (a Roman cross) to die under God's curse (Deut. 21:23). All this was a perfect fulfilment of Scripture. Although he could have called on twelve legions of angels to set him free, Jesus submitted to his heavenly Father's will and allowed Roman soldiers to nail him to a cross (Matt. 26:53).

WHAT JESUS DID?

Understanding the person of Jesus is necessary for an adequate understanding of what he did — in his life, death and resurrection. One way of considering the central elements of Jesus' ministry is to examine some of the major theological terms that are commonly used to describe them.

Atonement

Atonement refers to what Jesus did to bring sinners into union or right relationship with God. Our sin estranges us from the holy God and Jesus became obedient to the Father's will (John 6:38; Matt. 26:39) and took *our* death, sin, condemnation and hell upon himself. Jesus was able to do this because he 'had no sin' (2 Cor. 5:21) and was, there-fore, an acceptable sacrifice to make this union possible.

Our sin is now covered, or atoned for, by the blood of Jesus. It still covers us, daily, and it will cover us into the farthest future. Jesus is in heaven, at the place of power and authority, and his blood can cleanse from sin. As our great

High Priest, Jesus atoned for our sin through his blood. Just as in the Old Testament the scapegoat was sent into the wilderness each year by the high priest of Israel to signify that the sins of the people were carried away (Lev. 16), so Jesus was sent to earth to carry our sin away by his death, once and for all. When he was buried, our sin was buried with him. When he rose from the dead, the great victory over sin and death was won!

Love

The love of God for men and women is the *reason* for the atonement. There are many biblical passages that speak of God's love for his creation. Here are a few: 'For God so loved the world that he gave his one and only Son, that whoever believes in him shall not perish but have eternal life' (John 3:16); 'But God demonstrates his own love for us in this: While we were still sinners, Christ died for us' (Rom. 5:8); 'This is love: not that we loved God, but that he loved us and sent his Son as an atoning sacrifice for our sins' (1 John 4:10).

There is no 'why' for the love God has for us — it is unmerited and entirely because he *chooses* to love us. He loved us and he acted. His acting in Jesus was the fullest expression of his love, and the only possible expression of it. Nothing short of Jesus, the Son of God, dying in our place would satisfy the absolute demands of God's holiness and righteousness. God would not save any other way, could not save any other way; indeed, no other way was sufficient.

Sacrifice

Jesus' death was a sacrificial offering to God, who is offended by sin. The Old Testament sacrificial system, especially the sin offering, is the backdrop for the sacrifice of Jesus on the cross. Isaiah depicts the Messiah as taking the sin of the people upon himself, pouring out his life and becoming an offering for sin (Isa. 53:4–5,10,12). The whole of the Mosaic sacrificial system may be said to be a historical prophetic drama of what Jesus the Messiah would one day fulfil in his own sacrifice.

Substitution

When Jesus died on the cross, he died in our place — he was our substitute. Since no sin may come before God, if we are to be in the presence of God we must have our sin removed. We are absolutely powerless to forgive ourselves, or to do anything at all to remove sin. Jesus did what we can never do. He is the substitute. He died in our place. He died instead of us. He took our sin, our death and our everlasting punishment on himself.

Propitiation

Propitiation means that the death of Jesus, God the Son, satisfied the judgement of God the Father against sin and sinners. The absolute penalty against sin is death and eternal separation from God in hell. The sinless Son of God, a sacrifice without blemish, met the just demands of God and his law when he died on the cross. His atoning sacrifice propitiated, or legally qualified, as payment for our sin (Rom. 3:25; Heb. 2:17; 1 John 2:2; 4:10).

Reconciliation

Sin causes a separation between God and the sinner. God is holy and may not even 'look' upon sin. There is a hell because it is absolutely impossible for sin to come into the presence of God. Since we are all sinners, we are all alienated from God, completely shut off from him. In our unconverted state, we were 'dead in [our] transgressions and sins' (Eph. 2:1). However, in Christ we are reconciled to God — his cleansing blood is powerful enough to remove the sin that separates us from God. Paul described the reconciling ministry of Jesus in this way:

> Therefore, if anyone is in Christ, he is a new creation; the old has gone, the new has come! All this is from God, who reconciled us to himself through Christ ... not counting men's sins against them. And he has committed to us the message of reconciliation (2 Cor. 5:17–19).

Sin had built a wall, Jesus tore it down.

Redemption

Sin brings bondage to the sinner — we are captives to sin and death. Just like a slave, we cannot free ourselves. Jesus redeemed us; he bought us back. The price paid, the ransom price, was his own life: 'In him we have redemption through his blood, the forgiveness of sins' (Eph. 1:7). As our substitute, Jesus shed his blood on the cross and died because of, and for, our sin, and redeemed us from the bondage to sin.

And God was completely satisfied with the price Jesus paid for the redemption of all those who trust in him for their salvation. It was a perfect redemption!

Justification

Justification means to be declared righteous. Through Christ, we appear, in God's eyes, as if we had *never* sinned, not even once. The blood of Jesus washes away all our sin — the sin from the past, the present and even the future. This is freely done, without requiring any work on our part, nothing at all. The condemned, the walking dead, are set free. At one time we were awaiting the execution of our dreadful sentence for sin, but in Christ (as if granted a last-minute reprieve), we are declared righteous by the great Judge of the living and the dead. God actually sees us as perfect through his beloved Son, Jesus. This is amazing, unfathomable grace. This is love in all its purity.

Mediation

Jesus is the mediator (1 Tim. 2:5). He is the one who effects reconciliation between God and man. He did this by taking away, through his death, that which caused separation between us and God, namely, our sin. We cannot come before God the Father in our sinful condition. We must first come to Jesus, the Mediator, for cleansing. God the Son stands between us and God the Father. We must be 'in Christ' in order to come to the Father.

Jesus rose from the dead. On the third day after his burial, a Sunday morning, Jesus rose from the dead. He now lives for ever, interceding for us, pleading our case before the throne of God. He is the Mediator whose blood is always sufficient to cleanse us from our sin. This is the witness of Scripture; this witness has continued unchanged by the confessional and universal church down through history, and this is the witness of the converted today.

We are saved by grace (God's unmerited favour); it is God who saves us in Christ; salvation is not our own accomplishment — this we agree on. The Holy Spirit convicts us of our sin and our need of the Saviour. The Holy Spirit reveals Jesus to us. When we are born again, it is the Holy Spirit who gives birth to us (we cannot give birth to ourselves). In preaching and witnessing, therefore, we emphasize the person and work of Jesus. As Paul wrote: 'Faith comes from hearing the message, and the message is heard through the word of Christ' (Rom. 10:17). Jesus has completed his work; it is truly finished.

5

CONVERSION: THE SUBJECTIVE EXPERIENCE

Conversion is a personal, inner experience. Because of its subjective nature, it is difficult to analyze in concrete terms. Indeed, while every individual conversion is different, the objective aspects of conversion (considered in the previous chapter) remain the same: 'Jesus Christ is the same yesterday and today and for ever' (Heb. 13:8). Few points of theology are free from debate but the considerable discussion over the subjective aspects of conversion speaks much to the inherent mystery in it.

Webster's Dictionary defines 'mystery' as 'a religious truth that one can know only by revelation and cannot [be] fully understood'. By the mystery of conversion I mean that which resolves the space between God and man as illustrated in Michelangelo's painting, *The Creation* (referred to at the end of chapter two). The painting shows God and man with a gap between their extended fingers. Conversion is the mysterious bridging of that gap. This mystery is often uncomfortable for us to consider since it means acknowledging that the way conversion actually happens is beyond our understanding and control. For example, whatever the preacher of the gospel might do, he cannot give spiritual birth to someone or describe exactly how such a birth takes place. The best he can do after proclaiming the gospel message is to say, 'Believe in the Lord Jesus, and you will be saved' (Acts 16:31).

THE INNER EXPERIENCE

What goes on in the hearts and minds of people when the Spirit of God is at work is a mystery about which we can often only speculate. For me, as I have already described, I had a sense of being guilty before God. I sensed and felt inwardly that I was a sinner, separated from God. I also felt judged by the preacher and other Christians. I wanted to avoid them — but at the same time I was drawn to church to hear what I could. It was unusual behaviour on my part and something I probably could not have explained.

Even while I was feeling lost and judged, I was also attracted to Jesus. Of course, I had heard about Jesus for a long time and my friends and I would occasionally discuss religion, but this was entirely different. Without fully realizing what was happening to me, I had a strong inner sense that Jesus was the Saviour. I was simultaneously attracted and repelled. There was no one to discuss this with, even if I had had the vocabulary to express what was inside of me. For months and months, an inner battle went on inside my mind — until, in one moment, it was over and I 'suspected' that Jesus had saved me. What that looked like I cannot even explain now; I only sensed then that the inner warfare was finally over.

Charles Davenport lived across the street from me at the time and he also attended the Baptist church in Fairfield.

We argued all the time, mostly before my conversion but afterwards as well. I was very defensive as I tried to trap him with the clever questions I thought of in order to prove that his Christianity was nonsense. What shocks me now is that I even started to care about Christianity because I never had before. What got me going? With hindsight I can only say that it was the Father drawing me to the Son.

During this time, I was often defensive, protective and angry, and I have seen many others exhibit the same behaviour. Sadly, this is not always understood for what it is — a genuine seeking after God — and the result is that the seeker is not appreciated but rejected by the very ones who know the gospel. I have had many intense arguments or debates with people shortly before they were actually converted. Something was going on inside them that almost defies description, perhaps 'spiritual warfare' comes closest. It seems as though the devil, the enemy of God, and the whole of creation is actively involved in keeping people from Christ. Paul referred to it this way: 'The god of this age has blinded the minds of unbelievers, so that they cannot see the light of the gospel of the glory of Christ, who is the image of God' (2 Cor. 4:4).

The ultimate warfare is spiritual; heaven and hell hang in the balance, not simply physical life and death. Men and women are powerless and bound to lose a spiritual war except that Jesus has defeated the ancient enemy through his death and resurrection. This is what John meant when he wrote: 'The reason the Son of God appeared was to destroy the devil's work' (1 John 3:8).

THE UNIQUENESS OF CONVERSION

My conversion experience is not like anyone else's. Each conversion is unique, yet there are definite similarities and common threads running through conversion stories — *conviction of sin and a growing attraction to Jesus*. Some people become worried because they did not have a *dramatic* conversion experience; mine certainly was not. Some cannot say when they were converted while others know the very second the event occurred. Some wept, some laughed, some fell asleep exhausted as one might at the end of a long wrestling match. Some had simply a clear knowledge that they had been born again. Some describe their conversion as a huge weight being lifted from their shoulders. Many simply discover that something had to have happened because their wants and desires shifted — now the Bible, prayer, church, and anything to do with Jesus interested them.

Such was true of my conversion. The last place anyone would expect Mr 'Cool' Philpott to be was at church singing hymns with the completely 'un-cool' types who went to church. It was quite a discovery I made about what was happening to me, but I did not care. I only knew I was where I wanted to be. Even when I encountered opposition from my family and friends, though it would hurt, it was never enough to dissuade me from being a follower of Jesus.

Having been a pastor for a long time I can definitely testify that there are no 'cookie-cutter' conversions. Some people seem to have all kinds of troubles descend on them after their new birth. Others seem to have it easy for a considerable period of time only to be challenged later on, sometimes shaken deeply. Some will wander or slide away from the faith for a time, but come back, often with greater strength. Notorious sinners will be delivered from their sinful acts for a period and think they will never be tempted by those things again. But they will probably face that battle in the future. And so a Christian's experience, their coming to faith, their challenges and struggles, will vary from person-to-person but it will still be evident that they have been genuinely converted.

I like systems — clear methods, predictable outcomes, everything neat and tidy — but when it comes to conversion, I cannot predict the way the Holy Spirit will work in a person's life. Often Christians are tempted to try to identify and control how God goes about his business. We want there to be something, some system or method, and yet there is no biblical warrant for explaining away the mystery involved in conversion.

THE DANGER OF PRESCRIBING A METHOD WHEN SCRIPTURE DOES NOT

Paul and Silas did not give particular instructions to the Philippian jailer about the method by which he was to believe when he asked them, 'Sirs, what must I *do* to be saved?' They replied, '*Believe* in the Lord Jesus, and you will be saved.' The Greek verb translated 'believe' is an aorist imperative indicating that Paul and Silas *expected* the jailer to believe and be saved right then. Within the entire record of conversions in the New Testament, no method is ever set out. The message is: 'Repent, confess and believe.' There are no instructions about *the way* people are to repent, confess and believe.

'Nature abhors a vacuum', is a well-used adage. Indeed, I think human nature especially abhors a vacuum within a belief system. So, regarding conversion, many have filled in the apparent vacuum; we have come up with prayers, invitations and other mechanisms. Where does Scripture provide a prayer to be used in accepting Jesus? Where in Scripture does anyone come forward or raise a hand to accept Jesus?

People may be converted after saying a prayer, coming forward, raising their hand, or being baptized; any number of events may occur that may, in specific cases, lead to conversion. True conversion does not automatically follow, however, and certainly all of these customs lack clear biblical warrant. My belief is that there are people in our churches who think they are converted because they have performed one of these acts. And I believe these people are in danger. I would go further and say that I am convinced there are some pastors and ministers in our churches who think their own names are recorded in the Lamb's book of life when in fact they are not.

The objective aspects of conversion are generally incontrovertible points of biblical theology. I could proclaim these points even before I preached my first sermon. I thought that because I understood them I controlled the means by which people were converted. 'I had five decisions last Sunday', was a familiar boast. Without ever questioning my assumptions, I was quite sure that each one was truly born again. Of course, experience demonstrated that many of those 'decisions for Jesus' faded quickly away. Usually my facile excuse was: 'No follow-up.' This served to explain everything. In many cases, however, the progress of new 'converts' was followed up. They were baptized, they became members of our church and yet, over some issue, or as a result of some offence, they left and did not go to another church. 'No spiritual life; a flat line on the monitor,' I would say and chalk it up to the devil, or bring out some other excuse that helped to put it behind me.

Many of the matters covered in this book become clear when one preaches for conversion and asks people to be sure of their salvation. A preacher of the gospel will be amazed at the kind of trouble he will get into when he earnestly contends for people's salvation. Those who are truly converted will be glad (though not always at first) to be challenged about their salvation; those who think they are converted and are not will be very uncomfortable, and even angry. If a preacher affirms and confirms people, makes them feel positive about themselves and their church, he will be liked and praised. And so they all go to sleep, unaware of the false conversions.

WHAT CAN A PREACHER DO?

What can the gospel preacher do, then, beyond reciting, 'Believe in the Lord Jesus, and you will be saved'?

To believe in the Lord Jesus is to trust in him alone for forgiveness and salvation and to submit to him as Lord and Christ. Yes, this is the gospel. How does a person who is lost begin to trust Jesus? What should he or she do? I do not know. For twenty-nine years I thought I knew, but now I realize that there is no simple methodology to bringing about conversion.

C. H. Spurgeon would preach the gospel long and hard and give no invitation whatsoever. There was no hand-raising, no coming forward, no praying the sinner's prayer. He did invite people to come to see him or his deacons to discuss their conversion. Each person who joined his church was personally interviewed by Spurgeon about his or her conversion. Spurgeon urged those who were not converted to come to Jesus and trust him for salvation.

When we come to Jesus for forgiveness and salvation because the Holy Spirit has convicted us and shown us Jesus as the remedy, we look to Jesus — and not to any other person or institution — as the source of our salvation.

Is it wrong to give an invitation that asks people to come forward and accept Jesus as their Saviour and Lord? Even though most of the evangelical Christian world relies on the standard 'invitation' it is not a clear biblical practice. I will say, at the very least, that we should not assume that true conversion has occurred when we use such a method. Conversion is too mysterious and subjective to base the most important event of one's life on a simple prayer that has no biblical precedent. I prefer to emphasize coming to Jesus for forgiveness and salvation without suggesting any method whatsoever. This has proved to yield true conversions time after time.

Even the best process used by the most experienced minister will not guarantee a true conversion. The preacher must present the objective truth of the gospel and the Holy Spirit will apply that truth subjectively to the hearer of the Word in a way we do not understand and do not control.

6

SIGNS OF THE CONVERTED

We receive salvation by coming to Jesus for the forgiveness of our sin. We do this by God's mercy and grace and by the working of his Holy Spirit. Following conversion we are to do good works (Eph. 2:10) and the Holy Spirit operates in our lives so that *we will do* good works. As Colossians 1:29 puts it, Paul struggled, or strove 'with all his energy', yet it was God powerfully working in him that produced the kind of life and ministry that God had called him to. We do not begin by *faith* and end up *working for* God's continued favour and mercy (Gal. 3:3). These good works are considered to be evidence that we are truly born again; we can call them 'signs of the converted'. Since the Scripture does not give a succinct and complete list of the signs, and since they may be almost limitless, I will focus only on the most obvious ones.

There is no predictable sequence in which these signs appear in the life of a new convert. The Christian experience is not that simple. During the course of my ministry I have seen many variations. Some became zealous for evangelism from the start. Others could not get enough of the Bible. Still others loved to praise and worship the Lord above all else. Some spent long hours in prayer. Some new converts struggled with everything.

SIGNS FROM MY OWN EXPERIENCE

The model I will use to describe the signs of the converted is derived from my personal experience as a Christian, which may not be standard, but it is accessible.

A sense of peace and relief

A believer in Jesus may have the experience of an inner peace and sense of relief. For instance, I knew that I was lost and in danger of rejecting Jesus altogether. The moment after I came to Jesus I experienced a sense of being forgiven. Although it sounds like a cliché, it was as though a heavy burden had been lifted from me. At that time, I never told anyone how I felt — it was a private, inner experience. Probably 'joy' comes closest to describing what I felt. Never before had I thought about being thankful to God, but now I felt grateful to Jesus.

Baptism

A normative and important part of the Christian's life is baptism. Baptism is extremely important because it is the most natural step to take following conversion. Jesus instructed his apostles to baptize new converts and, as a result, the early Christians were baptized following their conversion. Baptism is an act of obedience, and a way to confess our faith in Jesus as Saviour in front of others. Over the years, I have found the conversion testimonies of so many to be faulty when they declared faith in Christ but refused baptism.

Identifying with Jesus

Jesus made it clear that his followers will confess, or acknowledge, their faith in him. He said, 'Whoever acknowledges me before men, I will also acknowledge him before my Father in heaven' (Matt. 10:32). And, in the very next verse, Jesus goes to say that the exact opposite would also hold true. Identifying with Jesus comes quite easily, as a new believer will have a new attitude towards him. Before conversion Jesus may be ignored, feared, dismissed, undervalued, and so on, but after conversion Jesus assumes a far different place in their thinking. He is now seen as their beloved Saviour, the one who died on a cross and shed his blood, all because of his love for sinners. A person who was once troubled by the mere mention of Jesus now finds he is attracted to that very name.

Developing a relationship with God

The essence of a Christian's life is his relationship with God. Communication is the heart of any human relationship and so it is with our relationship with God. The inspired Word of God is the chief way God communicates with us. A Christian does not hear the voice of God speaking to him, giving him direct personal messages, but the Holy Spirit applies to the believer's life, in ways largely unknown to us, truths from the Scripture. Prayer is the primary way we communicate back to God. A relationship emerges — slowly, steadily, not easily; and it develops throughout the Christian's lifetime. It is never perfect, and sometimes the quality of the relationship suffers, but it is never broken completely, despite our rebelliousness.

Bible reading may come easily for some Christians. For instance, early on I developed the daily discipline of reading two chapters from both the Old and New Testaments each day. Prayer, however, was more difficult. Some days I could pray for long periods at a time; on other days I could not settle down for even a minute or two. In the best of times my Bible reading inspires my praying and I cannot get enough of either. At other times, I may go for days, or even weeks, feeling dry and lifeless. Nevertheless, I have learned not to berate myself, or give up, in the 'dry seasons' but to press on with the relationship I have with God until he brings 'times of refreshing'.

Sin becomes really sinful

Our relationship with God is a purifying experience, 'because the Lord disciplines those he loves...' (Heb. 12:6; also see Rev. 3:19). When we are struggling with sinful behaviour in our lives our relationship with God will be affected. My sinful ways came to my attention as never before. I began to recognize that the coping mechanisms of rebellion that I had relied on to see me through stressful times were actually sinful. I was amazed; I was confused; I was humiliated; at times I was scandalized. When we try to stop sinning on our own, we usually fail and may think that the Christian life is not for us. Nevertheless, we slowly learn that sin is only overcome by relying on the finished work of Jesus and his righteousness.

There is a great paradox when it comes to the converted sinner and his sin. I refer to it as the 'perfect/sinner' paradox. We are supposed to be 'perfect'. Jesus said, 'Be perfect, therefore, as your heavenly Father is perfect' (Matt. 5:48). Perfection is the highest possible standard. It is not possible for a Christian to be perfect through his own effort; therefore, God has made us perfect *in Christ*.

The Christian is 'in Christ' and is whole and perfect before God, yet the Christian sins. The Apostle John wrote:

> If we claim to be without sin, we deceive ourselves and the truth is not in us. If we confess our sins, he is faithful and just and will forgive us our sins and purify us from all unrighteousness. If we claim we have not sinned, we make him out to be a liar and his word has no place in our lives (1 John 1:8–10).

The 'perfect' sinner confesses his sin and is forgiven. The paradox stands: 'perfect/sinner'.

John went on to say, 'My dear children, I write this to you so that you will not sin. But if anybody does sin, we have one who speaks to the Father in our defence — Jesus Christ, the Righteous One' (1 John 2:1). John holds up the standard and at the same time knows that his 'dear children' will sin. The Greek phrase could easily be translated: 'if anybody does sin, *and he will* '. John's solution to the sin problem is not to try harder, have more faith or pray harder. Nor does John use expressions that would shame his 'dear children', such as: 'What's the matter with you?' or 'You are an embarrassment to the faith!' or 'You are no good!' John points the sinning Christian to Jesus, the only One who is righteous.

Experiencing rejection for standing up for Jesus

Jesus said, 'Blessed are you when people insult you, persecute you and falsely say all kinds of evil against you because of me' (Matt. 5:11; see 1 Peter 4:12–17). Jesus expected his followers to suffer rejection because of him. These two things go together. When my old friends learned that I had 'got religion' I lost half of them immediately. They were angry that I would no longer participate in and tolerate the 'good old times'. They felt I was being accusatory and judgemental.

This is typical. Rejection cannot be avoided. The new believer quickly discovers who his real friends are.

Being in the fellowship of a church

The church is central to the Christian experience. At conversion we are placed by God in his universal church in which all living born-again believers are members. The local church is the normal 'spiritual home' of every believer. Occasionally a Christian may have trouble finding a suitable church, but it has been my experience that Christians will naturally seek out a body of believers to be with.

In the church we learn to worship, praise and serve God. Many of our 'rough edges' are rounded off as we fellowship and work with others. There is no perfect church or denomination, but each of us eventually finds a church that is good enough to call 'home'. It may take time, but the converted person will not rest until a church home is found. It is important for the believer to stick with his church, to attend as often as possible and to look for avenues of service within the context of the church. It is in the church that baptism should take place. It is in the church that we celebrate the Lord's Supper. Once in a while I meet a converted person who refuses to be involved in a church. Usually there is a long story that goes with it, yet I always urge such a person to put differences aside, exercise forgiveness, be willing to agree to disagree, find a church and become involved.

Witnessing to others about the gospel

There is no such thing as a secret disciple of Jesus. It is only natural to learn to share our faith in Jesus with others. We will want others to hear and understand the 'good news' of the gospel of Christ — those in our families, our friends, our co-workers, people across the world. We will not want to keep it to ourselves! The mature Christian will be sharing his faith with others in some way. Not all of us have the Holy Spirit's gift to become full-time preachers, but all are called by Jesus to be his witnesses.

Growing into the fulness of Christ

We are called to the very highest of standards — that is, to grow to maturity, 'to the whole measure of the fulness of Christ' (Eph. 4:13). Although this process is never completed in this life, the maturing of our faith in Jesus continues to develop over our lifetime. It can be a painful process. A long-term graph of the stocks that comprise the Dow Jones Industrial Average comes to mind. It has many ups and downs — some sharp rises and other sharp declines — but over the long term, it goes up. There may even be a crash. To use another metaphor, we may receive a body blow, but the athlete — and we are likened to athletes in Scripture — gets up off the floor and continues on. We deal with sin in our lives and cope with the frustrations of being in the world but not belonging to it (John 15:19). And as if that was not enough, we find that we are also engaged in spiritual warfare against evil forces (Eph. 6:10–20).

Learning to give

By nature we are self-centred takers, not givers. The gospel's call to give challenges us right to the core. We are called to give our money — the tithe being the standard, and offerings over and above that. We are called to be a thankful people. Our giving flows naturally out of gratitude for the richness of God's mercy towards us.

I recall how hard it was for me to give. I wish I could remember what motivated me to begin giving in the first place but learning to give was a pivotal element in my Christian growth and experience.

SIGNS OF THE CONVERTED FROM 1 JOHN

The Apostle John gave first-century Christians a description of the nature of the Christian life in the letter we call 1 John. A brief summary of John's teaching will serve as a useful conclusion to this chapter.

First, John says we know God (that is, we have been born again) if we obey his commands: 'We know that we have come to know him if we obey his commands' (1 John 2:3). The same truth is expressed a few verses later when the Apostle tells us, 'Whoever claims to live in him must walk as Jesus did' (1 John 2:6).

To obey Jesus' commands and walk as he did is described in terms of love, *agape* love. *Agape* is a word that comes directly from the Greek language of the New Testament. It is easier to say *what it is not* than what it is. It is not emotion or feeling-centred love; it is not desire or lust; it is not even a friendship kind of love. *Agape* love is acting toward another for his or her best interest. I think Jesus described it best when he said, 'Do to others what you would have them do to you, for this sums up the Law and the Prophets' (Matt. 7:12).

The Christian is to love his brother (1 John 2:10–11; 3:11; 4:7) and, conversely, he is not to 'love the world or anything in the world' (1 John 2:15). The Christian is not to continue in sin: 'No one who lives in him keeps on sinning. No one who continues to sin has either seen him or known him' (1 John 3:6).

John actually states the exact commands that the Christian is to obey: 'And this is his command: to believe in the name of his Son, Jesus Christ, and to love one another as he commanded us' (1 John 3:23). Perhaps the key wording is found in the last part of verse 24: 'We know it by the Spirit he gave us.'

The signs of conversion from 1 John may be summarized like this: *trusting in Jesus for salvation, loving our brothers and sisters and turning away from sin.* The unconverted will have no interest in these things; rather, such things will be despised. We know that we have been born again and that Jesus truly lives in us when these things are true in our lives — yet it is confirmed only by the Holy Spirit who indwells the believer. It is much as Paul stated in Romans 8:16: 'The Spirit himself testifies with our spirit that we are God's children.' A converted person will trust in Jesus for salvation, have a new attitude of love for others and desire to turn away from sin.

This is not an exhaustive list of all the signs that believers will display. Some of the more obvious signs were mentioned. If these signs are not evident after some period of time, then it would be good to examine whether in fact there has been a true conversion. This is not to say that *all* the signs must be present in the life of a Christian at any one time, or that they must all be functioning smoothly. From time to time I still struggle in my Christian life, and there has been a time or two when the warfare has been fierce, even to the point of losing a battle.

I do not want to intimate that the Christian life is just full of duty and work. It is the greatest privilege and pleasure to serve Jesus. There is nothing to compare with it — nothing at all! All else pales in comparison with serving and loving and worshipping the God of all creation.

CONCLUDING THOUGHTS

The signs or characteristics of genuine conversion occur supernaturally. Jesus' use of the term 'born again' in John 3 was no accident. Human growth and maturation has its counterpart, to some measure, in the believer's growing up into the fulness of Christ (Eph. 4:13). As a pastor I have spent many anxious times waiting for people in my congregation to begin to 'grow up'. They would mature but at their own rate, despite my efforts with various disciple-ship programs. My observation is that *God grows up his own children* however stubborn they might be. God begins a good work and *he completes it*; we are *his* workmanship.

7

FALSE CONVERSION: A BIBLICAL BASIS

In 1969 I was at a large church in New Mexico for a Sunday evening service. At the time I was part of the 'Jesus Movement'. That evening our group, *Joyful Noise*, sang and gave testimonies. At the conclusion of the meeting I issued a standard invitation. In response to the invitation, the pastor of that large, prosperous church walked down the aisle! He was twice my age and had been the pastor there for fifteen years. He whispered in my ear that he had never come to Jesus for salvation and he had just realized it that evening. Although he was embarrassed, he could not be put off. There we were, right in the front; no one else came forward. I prayed with that sincere, brave pastor and I hope he was genuinely born again that night.

How could such a strange thing happen? This man had obviously been baptized and had studied a considerable amount of theology during his seminary training. At his ordination examination, he would have been asked about his doctrine, call and conversion. He had preached the gospel hundreds of times and had issued hundreds of 'invitations' to his hearers to receive Jesus as Saviour. He had done all those things, yet was not truly converted.

I am not sure how this happened. Who can fully know the spiritual workings in another person's life? Nevertheless, there had been no true conversion for that pastor. I have observed the same in many others — pastors, elders and church members. And if you are the pastor of a church, or a Christian who has been faithful in a church over an extended period of time, you have observed false conversions too.

THE PARABLE OF THE SOWER

The Scripture anticipates the possibility of false conversion. In the parable of the sower (Mark 4:1–20) Jesus describes four places where a farmer sowed his seed: along the path, in rocky places, among thorns and in good soil. Jesus explains that the seed is a metaphor for the word, which is the message of the gospel.

Jesus said that some people are like seed that is sown along the path. The word is sown but as soon as people hear it Satan takes it away. Could any of these experiences have been mistaken for conversion? I think so. We often hear people say they used to go to church, but later they became Muslims or Buddhists, etc. Or we hear others say that they have had fantastic religious experiences in church, or on a mountain peak. Some even report 'seeing God' while they were in a drug-induced state. Still others say they felt the presence of God while they were having some kind of transcendental experience. In every case, there was some kind of religious or mystical experience. Can these be true conversions to Jesus? After all, something 'spiritual' or 'religious' happened! I believe they have experienced false conversion.

In the second instance (seed falling on rocky places) the word is heard and there is an immediate response. Jesus says, they 'receive it with joy' (Mark 4:16). But there is no root or depth to their response and when trouble or persecution comes because of the gospel, they 'quickly fall away' (Mark 4:17). Was this true conversion? No, there was an experience of some kind, but not conversion.

In this instance, there is a falling away that occurs. In the Greek text, *skavdalizovtai* means 'to be offended' and is translated 'fall away' in the NIV. These people are offended because they experience trouble and persecution because of the gospel. Their initial 'joy' is not able to sustain them through these challenges. I have often seen this. People weep, carry on, come forward, fall down, repeat the sinner's prayer and praise enthusiastically. But often they never come back or show any further interest. When I attempt to follow up with them, they apologize and make excuses and promises. However, they are rarely seen again. What happened? A false conversion.

Unless we realize that false conversions do occur, we will not be able to help people who think they have been converted. These 'converts' have a profound religious experience but then might ask, 'Is that all there is?' When friends, family or other associates abuse them because of Jesus and the Word, they easily and quickly walk away. Often such people say to me, 'This path is not for me.' These people are unaware that they did not experience true conversion.

In the third set of circumstances (the seed sown among thorns) the word is heard, 'but the worries of this life, the deceitfulness of wealth and the desires for other things' result in a life that is unfruitful (Mark 4:19). These people are like plants that grow but become choked by weeds so that they fail to bear fruit. And where there is no fruit, there is no conversion. While Christians may indeed go through *times* of unfruitfulness, a persistent unfruitfulness must be taken as a sign that there has been no true conversion. This is substantiated by Jesus in Matthew 7:16–20, where he concludes, 'Thus, by their fruit you will recognize them', and in John 15:8 where he says, 'This is to my Father's glory, that you bear much fruit, showing yourselves to be my disciples.'

In the fourth case (seed sown in good soil) the word was heard, accepted and produced a crop 'thirty, sixty or even a hundred times what was sown' (Mark 4:20). Obviously, this is a description of a person who has experienced true conversion. The word is planted in their heart, it takes root, it bears up under trials and persecution and their life begins to bear godly fruit.

JESUS' WARNING IN THE SERMON ON THE MOUNT

Jesus himself warns about the possibility of false conversion in the Sermon on the Mount:

> Not everyone who says to me, 'Lord, Lord,' will enter the kingdom of heaven, but only he who does the will of my Father who is in heaven. Many will say to me on that day, 'Lord, Lord, did we not prophesy in your name, and in your name drive out demons and perform many miracles?' Then I will tell them plainly, 'I never knew you. Away from me, you evildoers!' (Matt. 7:21–23).

Jesus is speaking of people who certainly do not *appear* to be against him. They address him as 'Lord' and have carried out 'power' ministry in his name. Jesus indicates that many people will assume they have salvation when they do not. These people will hear the saddest words that can ever be spoken: 'I never knew you. Away from me, you evildoers!' This text motivated me to begin preaching conversion-oriented sermons, as I was horrified to think that members of my own congregation might one day hear those damning words. Yes, I knew it would be a shock and challenge to some in my congregation, and I knew that church membership would shrink. Nevertheless, I felt it was my responsibility to present the gospel message so that people would either see their lost condition and come to Jesus or, if they were already converted, become assured of their salvation.

PAUL'S FAREWELL TO THE EPHESIAN ELDERS

The Apostle Paul was keenly aware of the danger of false conversions. When he was on his way to Jerusalem, he asked the elders of the Ephesian church to meet with him at the coastal town of Miletus. Part of what he said to the elders included this warning: 'I know that after I leave, savage wolves will come in among you and will not spare the flock. Even from your own number men will arise and distort the truth in order to draw away disciples after them' (Acts 20:29–30).

The Ephesian church would face two threats, one external and the other internal. 'Savage wolves' were the *external threat*. They would come into the church from the outside. This is clearly indicated by the use of the Greek word *eis*, which is translated in the NIV as 'come in', and means 'into'. The wolves would come into the church itself. How could 'wolves' get in? Through false conversion! Would these 'wolves' have been baptized? Would they have participated in the Lord's Supper? Would they have been accepted as a part of the church family? It would seem so, for Paul says they would come into the church. And how could 'wolves' come *into* the church except by false conversion?

Those who 'distort the truth' constituted the *internal threat*. They would arise from within the church and draw away disciples. Although this is not plainly stated in the text, my supposition is that these distorters of the truth would have some standing in the Ephesian church

— perhaps as teachers. Whether leaders or not, they would have been inside the church. How could they get into the church except on the basis of false conversion? This may have been due to a misunderstanding of what true conversion really is.

What pastor of any experience has not seen similar circumstances about which Paul warns the Ephesian elders? Paul's warning does not say whether 'wolves' and those who 'distort the truth' are converted or not. It is true that genuine Christian converts struggle, experience setbacks and even go through serious rebellion — these struggles do not necessarily mean they are unconverted. I would hold, however, to a high view of conversion and say that when Paul speaks of 'wolves' and those who 'distort the truth' he does not see them as genuine converts; he views them as enemies of the church and, therefore, enemies of God.

PAUL'S COMMENTS ON THE CHURCH AT CORINTH

Paul also assumed that there were false converts in the Corinthian church. He wrote, 'No doubt there have to be differences among you to show which of you have God's approval' (1 Cor. 11:19). There were divisions in the church and they were evident when the congregation met to celebrate the Lord's Supper. The key word, 'approval' (the Greek *dokimoi*) means 'approved by a test', 'tried and true' or 'genuine'. 'Approval,' in its common usage in English, does not carry the full force of the original Greek. I believe Paul was saying that there were those who were part of the Corinthian church who were not genuinely converted, approved of God or tried and true; yet they were in the church. They would, no doubt, have made a public confession of their faith in baptism. It is well known that the Corinthian church had many problems, and one reason may have been that some of those who were active in the daily life of the church were not converted.

JOHN'S WARNING OF 'ANTICHRISTS'

The Apostle John, in his first epistle, writes of the reality of false conversion:

> Dear children, this is the last hour; and as you have heard that the antichrist is coming, even now many antichrists have come. This is how we know it is the last hour. They went out from us, but they did not really belong to us. For if they had belonged to us, they would have remained with us; but their going showed that none of them belonged to us (1 John 2:18–19).

These 'many antichrists' had been part of the church. They were those who departed doctrinally from the church's position on the person and work of Jesus Christ. If they had truly belonged to the church, they would not have left. So how did they get into the church in the first place? I believe they had experienced false conversion — a conversion so close to the real thing that the church was not able to detect it without John's explanation.

It is thought that the antichrists to whom John refers were Gnostics. This group had a different system of beliefs and they were adept at incorporating Christian terminology and models into their heretical system. They could repeat creedal statements, be baptized and even make confessions of faith in Jesus by changing (in their own minds) the true meaning of the words and doctrines. The church mistook what they thought was doctrinal orthodoxy for conversion.

We often do the same today. People may have an orthodox theology, a conservative view of the Bible, a moral life, and so on, but these things do not always mean that conversion has taken place. And ministers often think it is enough to have right belief and upright behaviour. Approving doctrine and living a moral life are 'works' which do not produce or guarantee salvation; rather, they may only imitate a genuine conversion.

And so, Scripture repeatedly warns us about false conversion. In the next two chapters we will look at how false conversions occur.

8

HOW DO FALSE CONVERSIONS OCCUR?

It was the singer/songwriter Bob Dylan who said that we will serve somebody — 'it may be the devil or it may be the Lord'‡ — but we will serve somebody.

The people of the world are very religious. The Creator made us that way so that we might seek after him and find him (Acts 17:22–27). Religious concerns dominate the record of human history. People worship different gods for many reasons. With all the cults and theological confusion around us, who can doubt that 'conversions' to strange and false gods occur?

It is God's Holy Spirit working to bring a person into a saving relationship with Jesus Christ that accomplishes

---

‡ Bob Dylan, 'Gotta serve somebody', Album: *Slow Train Coming*, Columbia Records, 1979.

true Christian conversion. False conversions are those that seem to imitate this but do not have their focus on saving faith in Jesus. But how do these false conversions occur?

CRISIS CONVERSIONS

A crisis in our lives may predispose us emotionally and spiritually for a false conversion. There may be a death in our family, a terminal illness, a house fire, a flood or tornado that destroys everything, a divorce and the fracturing of our family life, the loss of our job — such a crisis may touch many of our lives sooner or later. Then, while our defences are down and we are very hurt or needy we may listen to someone or some group that claims to have all the answers. In desperation we welcome whatever is offered and relax, sheltered from the storm and turmoil of our life. It may be a secular, anti-Christian, cultic or mainstream Christian message. In the midst of crisis, we may lose our ability to think critically. Many of us will grasp on to anything that relieves our pain, sense of loss or confusion.

Crises brought about by drug and alcohol abuse and/or sexual misconduct (occurring primarily among adolescents and young adults) are responsible for the majority of false conversions in evangelical and charismatic Christianity. This may be illustrated by what often occurred in the Jesus Movement. The Jesus Movement was an awakening among counter-culture young people ('hippies') and middle-class Catholics and Protestants (the Catholic version of the Jesus Movement is often termed the Charismatic Renewal). Many large and successful ministries and churches emerged from the Jesus Movement and I was a leader in one such ministry in the San Francisco Bay area. These ministries and churches offered an opportunity for a new life through an extensive support system. Their process of conversion usually followed this course: the person in crisis came into direct contact with a member of a group comprised of those who had similar troubles in the past, the newcomer was heartily embraced and given a conditional acceptance. He was then challenged to repent from sin and rebellion. The newcomer could resolve the tension when he conformed to the desires of the group and thereby receive their full approval, love and support. This process was cemented by his 'acceptance of Jesus', baptism and formal membership in the group.

The 'testimony' given by such a person was primarily focused on the contrasts between his old and new life. For example, he may have testified that he was 'once a doper, an addict, a deadhead, an alcoholic...' and so on. There may be no question that such a person had altered his life for the better. However, his testimony did not centre on Jesus and the cross. Rather, his focus was on the group and the changes in his own behaviour and/or feelings.

Testimonies of life-enhancement are common with many groups, be they religious, political, educational, psychotherapeutic or commercially-based sales and motivational groups. If someone is no longer a despairing addict, does it necessarily mean that they have been genuinely converted? It could be that complex psychological, emotional or social forces motivated them to change their life.

Certainly, I am glad for any improvement in a person's life but I am more interested in whether this 'recovered' person has been converted. Our society applauds upright living, good citizenship, respectable action, family stability, honesty, kindness and love, whether these admirable qualities are the result of the gospel of Christ or not. Consequently, Christian leaders may fall into the trap of accepting upright behaviour in place of true conversion.

During my ministry I have not always recognized that people in crisis are vulnerable to false conversion. But experience has shown me that many crisis conversions do not last. Sometimes a person in crisis truly comes to Jesus after the Holy Spirit reveals to them their lost condition and need of a Saviour. In other situations this is not the case at all. I have prayed the sinner's prayer with some and led them in a confession of the risen Christ as their Saviour and Lord. Often baptism and church membership followed. When the effects of the crisis had diminished, however, the person appeared to walk away from Christianity. In reality, neither of us had recognized that there had been no true conversion — certainly not the person over whom I had pronounced: 'You are now born again.' I cannot undo the mistakes I made, but I am now acutely aware of how vulnerable people in crisis are to false conversion.

MORAL CONVERSIONS

It is good and right to embrace moral values and practice healthy living. Many people have discovered that the alternative is eventually disastrous. In nearly every segment of society, living a clean and moral life is applauded. The question we must ask is: 'If I live well, does that make me a Christian?' The clear, biblical answer is a resounding 'No'!

Living according to biblical principles may Christianize me, but it cannot make me a genuine Christian. In fact, a person who is able to persuade himself that he is living a commendable life may suppose that he does not need a Saviour at all. Such was the case of one particular man long ago.

Jesus told the story of two men: a Pharisee, a very clean man, and a tax collector, who in the eyes of his peers was a very unclean man. In fact, Luke introduced the story this way: 'To some who were confident of their own righteousness and looked down on everybody else, Jesus told this parable' (Luke 18:9). The story commences with these two men going to the temple in Jerusalem to pray. The Pharisee, a religious man, boasted about his scrupulous observance of the traditions of the elders of Judaism. The tax collector, however, 'beat his breast', perhaps out of a sense of personal loathing, and could only pray, 'God, have mercy on me, a sinner.'

Jesus' response in Luke 18:14 is astonishing: 'I tell you that this man [the tax collector], rather than the other [the Pharisee], went home justified before God.' Despite the clean living, the Pharisee only managed to deceive himself.

I am continually meeting people who think that Christianity is only about living a good life and helping other people. These things are important but they do not make you a Christian. Our works can never cause us to merit heaven or take away the sin that separates us from God. Only the payment of our sins through the blood of Christ is powerful enough to accomplish that. Many people possess strong moral standards but have not experienced the new birth — that will be all that matters when we stand before the righteous Judge.

'SPIRITUAL' CONVERSIONS

As a young man I had what I thought were miraculous experiences. One such experience was surviving a horrific car crash. My life, as is often said, did in fact 'flash before my eyes'. I took it as a sign that God was protecting me and that I must be on good terms with my Maker.

Others report similar experiences: an angel guided them, a spiritual presence appeared to them, a miracle of healing saved them, incredible coincidences took place that *had* to be of a spiritual origin, and so on. The result was the idea that they are somehow approved by God.

People who had been atheists have been known to suddenly switch to theism due to an extraordinary spiritual event, perhaps in a séance or through contact with a medium or fortune-teller. The proverbial 'foxhole religion' (eg. 'If I live through this, I'll go to church...') is generally short-lived. Regardless of the source or nature of the spiritual experience, some will take false comfort from it.

We must remember that the Holy Spirit *always and only* points to Jesus Christ. Other unholy spirits will only mislead, deceive and distract. A spiritual encounter is not in itself a converting or saving event; at best it is only a preliminary sign.

INSTITUTIONAL CONVERSIONS AND DENOMINATIONAL AFFILIATIONS

This form of false conversion rests on the authority of a religious or church organization. These organizations may baptize, which is the usual rite, or christen, initiate or confirm. People depend on the 'magic' of the institution to perform rituals and ceremonies that are said to have the power to forgive, save, enlighten or bring a person into the presence of God. As long as the religious act has been performed, despite any other consideration, people rely entirely upon the authority of the institution or denomination.

We also hear people say: 'I am a Baptist' or 'I am a Catholic' or 'I am a Methodist'. In the USA and the UK, a high percentage of people are baptized as infants. They naturally adopt at least a nominal allegiance to whatever denomination or church did the baptizing. And these church or denominational affiliations may pose a substantial barrier to a person's true conversion.

Often family tradition and fear may be the glue that holds a person to a religious group; they may never have evaluated their affiliation. Such a person may have little or no idea of how one becomes a Christian or that being a Christian is not just kind actions and a loving attitude — it is a life that is transformed by a personal relationship with God brought about through trust in Jesus for the forgiveness of sin.

A person who attempts to stake a claim in the kingdom of heaven on the basis of denominational affiliation or baptism has not been truly converted. Scripture is abundantly clear on this point. Rituals, priestly injunctions, 'holy' water or magical procedures cannot bring salvation. Yet people submit to these rites out of fear — fear of losing the salvation that they were told belongs only to their particular religious tradition. They also fear the loss of family, friends and status, which is often anchored on their original religious affiliation.

DOCTRINAL CONVERSIONS

The Christian world-view and the doctrines of Scripture are compelling. Dominant, sophisticated cultures have been under-girded by Christian faith and practice for centuries. Many of those raised in a 'Christian culture' may absorb the main tenets of Christianity but this is not the same as genuine conversion. They may have intellectually embraced orthodox Christian doctrine but remain unconverted. They usually do not understand the difference either.

In my view, this is one of the greatest problems to face those raised in cultures dominated by Christianity. Typically, in North America, the United Kingdom and most of Western Europe, doctrinal conversions are bound to occur. In the long run, it leads to spiritual erosion in the main Christian churches. It is a case of having the *form* of religion but not the *substance* — and the downhill slide is inevitable. Our churches may be full but there are many who are unconverted and unaware of their true condition — this is indeed tragic.

CULTIC CONVERSIONS

There are many cults and sects that have Christian links. They are distinguished by the fact that they tend to identify salvation, therefore conversion, as dependent on membership in their group and adherence to their theology or set of beliefs. A kind of 'conversion' does occur when new people struggle with the claims of the group and then, due to many and varied reasons, decide to become members and embrace the claims and ideology of the cult. This is sometimes described as a 'bending of the mind'.

Christian conversion is different. It is not giving up and submitting to a group's doctrine, certain rites and rituals, or the influence of family, society, or personal pressures, Christian conversion is being called by God and irresistibly drawn to Jesus Christ and the cross. Christian conversion is not faith in an institution or its ministers; it is not merely belief in certain doctrines or a group; it is not submission to a way of life either. It is trusting in Jesus — trusting that he has forgiven and saved you.

A BIRTHRIGHT

We hear people say: 'I am an American' or 'I am a Russian' or 'I am an Englishman'. These are examples of identities that are usually acquired at birth. Some people also believe that their birthright as Americans, for instance, automatically makes them Christians. After all, if they were not born Muslim, Hindu, Buddhist, Jewish and so on, then they must be Christian. This is what I thought. I assumed that being an American (a member of a 'Christian' nation) made me a Christian. Few pastors and ministers would accept such a basis for conversion.

Our birthright, however, can become a major impediment to the *new* birth brought about solely by the Holy Spirit of God. Some Jewish friends of mine, for instance, are sure they could never, or *should* never, believe in Jesus because they are Jewish. These are impressed with the idea that true Jews just don't believe in Jesus. The same could be said of a Muslim, Buddhist or Hindu. However, a Jew may become a Christian, as may a Muslim, a Buddhist, a Hindu, or whatever 'religious birthright' he or she might have. We are not permanently fixed to the religious identity we start out with in life. Faith in Jesus Christ is open to all (Rom. 1:16). He is the Saviour of the world. We always have in mind those most gracious words: 'For God so loved the world...'(John 3:16). *Any and all* may trust in him for the forgiveness of their sin.

EVANGELISM OF CHILDREN

Some popular evangelism techniques that are directed at children may also result in false conversions.

As a child, I had 'accepted' Jesus many times. I remember Mrs B who conducted vacation Bible schools every summer in the Portland, Oregon, neighbourhood where I grew up. She was a large person with a big voice and aggressive ways. She would gather up the children and take us to her house for Bible stories, songs, biscuits and a fizzy drink. I recall the black, red and white felt hearts displayed on the flannel board she had set up in her living room, one felt heart laid on top of the next. First, there was the black heart, the sinful heart which we did not want, since we could not go to heaven with a black heart. Next, there was the red heart, which was formerly the black heart, but now it was coated with the blood of Jesus. Then there was the white heart, the one we wanted, since we could not go to heaven and be with Jesus unless we had a white heart. There was not one child who did not want a white heart, so we prayed to be washed in the blood of Jesus. Mrs B made sure every one of us prayed; every summer my brothers and I would pray for a white heart so we could go to heaven.

I believe what my brothers and I experienced were *introjections* rather than conversions. Introjections occur when someone, in the presence of a powerful person or group, feels very anxious and reduces his anxiety by conforming to the expectations of that person or group. He does not realize that his new beliefs are motivated by an unconscious desire to relieve the tension produced by anxiety. Mrs B wanted to make sure we would go to heaven — so she scared the wits out of us! If we did not have a white heart we would go to hell. As children, we were scared that we would not only disappoint Mrs B, but that we would also burn in the devil's hell. As a result, she notched up a good number of 'conversions'.

I am concerned that ministers and pastors may be offended by my ideas. The problem is, if you abandon the traditional invitation, the sinner's prayer and simplistic child evangelism, what will happen to your ministry? Indeed, I had the same problem. For nearly thirty years, I operated with this evangelical model: I used the standard invitation and the sinner's prayer. Although I found that conversions did not automatically happen, I did not know what else to do. I did not appreciate the actual process of conversion. It took me well over a year of preaching on conversion to alter the traditional model in the church where I am pastor. Each week was a struggle because I did not have the usual conclusion to my sermon — that being the standard invitation. Through my newsletters and other means, I let the congregation know what I was working through and I asked them for their prayers and understanding.

'I PRAYED TO ACCEPT JESUS'

One day, in a Baptist church service, I 'came forward' in response to the invitation by the pastor; I then prayed the sinner's prayer with a deacon. Despite this, I was not converted. According to what Hank Hanegraaff has written (quoted at the beginning of chapter 2) I should have been converted. What happened?

I recited a prayer that acknowledged my situation, but I did not understand it. I did not see my lost condition nor realize that my sins had separated me from God. Do you think I was going to baulk right there in front of 300 people? No! I was going to pray whatever it was that deacon told me to pray. I was so new to the gospel that I understood little about Jesus or the significance of the cross. A heretic of the lowest order could have simply told me, 'Jesus is from Venus, and he came here on a spaceship.' Who was I to argue? There had been no revelation to me by the Holy Spirit of my particular need for salvation. All of this slowly dawned on me over the next six months. More than likely, my initial experience is very much aligned with the 'conversions' of the many who have 'come forward' in church services.

Frequently I hear ministers say that 'x' number of people accepted Christ at their Sunday service. When I inquire further, I am told that they came forward in response to an invitation and then prayed with someone. Sometimes people merely raised their hands to indicate that they were accepting Christ. Often the sermon had little to do with the heart of the gospel and the need for conversion. If any follow-up session occurred, the topic was usually baptism, church membership or some other tangential issue. Why is conversion taken so lightly? Is conversion always as simple as saying a little prayer or raising a hand?

These standard invitations to acknowledge acceptance of Jesus are traditional — even expected — in many Christian groups. My view is that we are making conversion out to be something easy and comfortable. These practices, while traditional in our churches, are without biblical precedent — and we must have the courage to abandon unbiblical practices. Why do I make what seems to be such a harsh and, yes, even judgemental statement? Because so many people in evangelical churches have recited a prayer, were baptized and have become members of a church without ever being converted! Unless God intervenes in their lives to show them their true state, these people will certainly hear Jesus say, 'I never knew you. Away from me, you evil-doers!' Preachers of the gospel must have a greater desire for the lost to be converted and to enjoy God's love for ever, than to see their church pews fill up.

THE ORIGINS OF THIS TYPE OF EVANGELISM

How did the evangelical church come to use methods like coming forward and reciting the sinner's prayer? I touched on this briefly in my introduction to this book but now let us consider this more fully.

In his *Revival Lectures*, the renowned revivalist of the mid-nineteenth century, Charles G. Finney, powerfully influenced evangelical Christianity. Many people were born again into the kingdom of God through his long ministry. However, he taught that a person could choose to accept Jesus at any time. Finney taught 'decisionism', which emphasizes man's capacity to accept Jesus as Saviour apart from the working of the Holy Spirit in conviction of sin and the revelation of Jesus to the spiritually blind. Finney invented what we know as 'the altar call' and 'the sinner's prayer'. Finney's apparent success influenced many others to imitate his methods. In a relatively short time Finney's 'New Measures', as they were known, strongly affected the heart and soul of evangelical Christianity.

Finney's influence is evident in the ministries of many of the great American evangelists from D. L. Moody to Billy Graham. They have taught that all a person needs to do is come forward, pray a (theologically correct) sinner's prayer and — just like that — he or she is converted. Although I acknowledge that some *are* genuinely converted, I challenge their assumptions about the process of conversion. Many people come forward for spurious reasons. They are often emotionally confused and feel pressure to recite the prayer. Evangelists from Charles Finney to Billy Graham have readily acknowledged that all who come forward and recite the sinner's prayer are not necessarily converted. Yet the standard model persists.

While working on the revision of this chapter I attended a gospel concert. The opening piece was 'I have decided to make Jesus my choice'. A mass choir delivered a powerful, magnificent rendition; the audience was greatly moved. I hummed along too, but as the evening wore on the words of that song began to trouble me. 'Decided' and 'choice'— this was how so many view the way you become a Christian. Is this true? Can someone spiritually blind, deaf, dumb, and dead in their sins, make a decision and a choice? Do we have that kind of control over our eternal future? Evidently the author of that song and many in the choir and the audience thought so. The song communicated a kind of boastfulness — 'See what I did! I chose Jesus' — that celebrates the human will and makes light of the will of God. But worse than that, it deludes those who have decided to choose Jesus into thinking they have been converted when all they have done is make a decision.

THE CHURCH-GROWTH MOVEMENT

I have attended several seminars on church growth. They focused on various techniques which you can use to get new people into your church. I also regularly receive materials announcing workshops or seminars that claim they can help me double the size of my congregation by some method or another. These methods include contacting people by cold-calling, mailing out a series of brochures and flyers or giving a series of sermons featuring self-help topics such as 'How to be successful in a crazy world'. I am advised to preach positive sermonettes that will inspire, uplift and help new-comers to feel welcome. Sermons that might be considered negative should be avoided, especially ones that mention sin, hell and the exclusiveness of Jesus.

The idea is that the Sunday morning 'celebration' is intended to be like a funnel into which are poured the maximum number of people. The gospel is not presented in these large gatherings; it is only presented in small groups, usually called cell groups — the bottom of the funnel. By the time newcomers make it to one of these groups they have been more thoroughly prepared for conversion through various levels of social and psychological bonding.

When I read about these church-growth strategies, I am reminded of cult recruitment techniques. Typically a cult's public meetings have a hidden agenda (especially when the cult has received bad press); the cult puts its best foot forward, leaving more controversial issues for small-group situations where some bonding has already taken place. When a Christian church does not proclaim the gospel in its public worship services and only evangelizes newcomers in its cell groups, it reminds me of these kinds of recruitment tactics. Yet these strategies seem to work! Statistics clearly indicate that by using church-growth techniques, you can increase the membership of your church. It seems hard to argue with success.

All across America churches are energetically recycling Christians who are constantly searching for the church that offers the best range of activities. If churches do not get on the bandwagon with these methods, they will lose out. Other churches will attract new people, perhaps from your congregation, if you do not employ positive celebrations, modern choruses with bands, lead singers and special praise groups, great activities for children and self-help groups for every dysfunction under the sun. Unconverted people who are looking to improve their lives *may* seek out a church that promises great things to those who join its congregation. Although their lives may be enhanced (with families strengthened, careers augmented and new friends acquired), the most important issue of life, salvation, may be entirely missed.

The methodology of the church-growth movement may result in false conversions when churches want to make it easy for people to become members. Preachers may shy away from strong gospel messages to avoid being 'offensive'. A preacher who uses a straightforward presentation of the need for conversion may not be as outwardly 'successful' as someone who is a church-growth practitioner. Church-growth techniques seem to work while preaching a straightforward gospel message often drives people away. I have found that if a conversion-oriented sermon is preached, those who are merely Christianized may not come back. Those who are satisfied with their own righteousness will baulk at the truth, which declares that they must either come to Jesus and his cross for forgiveness, or else they will be lost for ever.

Some churches, unhappily, attempt to convince people of their righteousness and membership in the kingdom of God — hoping to gain members and keep old members from straying. I did so and I see others doing it. It is vital to remember what C. H. Spurgeon said: 'The audience is not in the pews; the audience is in heaven.'

The tragic fact is false conversions do occur. But what is the nature of true conversion? And, how can we more carefully understand the nature of false conversion? Let us now turn our attention to the common experiences of true and false conversions.

9

EXPERIENCES TYPICAL OF TRUE AND FALSE CONVERSIONS

For the sake of clarity, I will outline my understanding of a classical conversion. By 'classical' I mean a view of conversion that has become standard among Christians down through the ages. I have read many testimonies of conversion. Each story is unique but there are common threads that run through them — this is what I mean by 'classical'.

Not all Christians will see their conversions as fitting into the model I present here. We are usually not conscious of a conversion 'process'; only in hindsight do we discern the events that lead to our salvation, and then sometimes only dimly.

TRUE CONVERSION — A CLASSICAL MODEL

Conversion begins when God reaches out to us and seeks us out. God's Holy Spirit reveals to us our lost condition.

The Holy Spirit convicts us of our sin and shows us that we stand guilty before a holy God. God's Spirit shows us that we are unable to save ourselves. Our religious acts and good works do not bring us salvation. We see that we are without hope.

By God's Spirit we see our need of the Saviour. We now begin to have an interest in Jesus. Conversion occurs, mysteriously through the Holy Spirit, as we come to Jesus for forgiveness and salvation.

Now we encounter the mystery of conversion. The Scripture says, 'Believe in the Lord Jesus, and you will be saved — you and your household' (Acts 16:31). *How* we believe in Jesus is not explicitly set forth in the Scriptures — no method of conversion is supplied. When Scripture is silent about something we should not make up something to 'fill the void'. Therefore, any set mechanism (such as saying the sinner's prayer) eliminates the mystery of conversion. (See chapter 2 for a fuller discussion of the mystery of conversion.)

Many conversions, although certainly not all, may look something like the following. We come to Jesus as we might come to any person — we approach him and speak with him. Jesus, God the Son, is in heaven at the right hand of the throne of God the Father so we come to him in prayer and we speak with him. The lost person, guilty and hopeless, comes to a loving Saviour who is eager to accept and forgive him. It is a personal communication enabled and empowered by the Spirit of God. In conversion, the work of the entire Trinity is evident.

Conversion, from a human vantage point, does not fit into easily defined moulds. Many conversion experiences occur when a convicted and awakened sinner prays for forgiveness. Other conversions are far different.

The conversion of John Wesley was a long and agonizing process. At a meeting in Aldersgate Street in London someone was reading from Martin Luther's preface to the Epistle to the Romans. In this preface, Luther describes how the heart is changed through faith in Christ. Wesley, reflecting on the moment, wrote in his journal: 'I felt my heart strangely warmed. I felt I did trust in Christ, Christ alone for salvation; and an assurance was given me that he had taken away my sins, even mine, and saved me from the law of sin and death.'

Charles Spurgeon was a spiritually despondent teenager, very much aware of his sinfulness and need of forgiveness. He was converted on hearing a Primitive Methodist lay preacher, an uneducated man, address him from the pulpit with the words: 'Young man, look to Jesus Christ!' (See Appendix II for the full account in Spurgeon's own words).

EXPERIENCES ASSOCIATED WITH FALSE CONVERSIONS

False conversions may also begin with a 'religious' or 'spiritual' experience and they often occur in church (even in Bible- and Christ-centered churches).

'Feeling the Spirit'

In churches where there is an emphasis on 'feeling the Spirit', people may mistake 'spiritual' experiences for conversion. A person may suppose that he is approved by God because he appears able to interact with the 'Spirit'. He may have a sensation of being brushed by angel's wings, or jolted by a spiritual power. Perhaps oil drips onto his open Bible. Perhaps he 'smells the sweet aroma of the Lord'. Perhaps he falls down 'under the power'. He may even 'laugh in the Spirit'. If the person comes into contact with something 'spiritual' and feels that he is approved by God, then he may easily view himself as a Christian. However, if that person has never come to Jesus for salvation, he is still unconverted and lost despite these 'spiritual' experiences.

The experience of awe

In the marketplace of spiritual disciplines and practices, there are many new, exciting and alluring types of spirituality. Almost everyone claims to be spiritual these days. There are powerful spiritual forces operating along many 'spiritual paths' that may convince someone that he has 'found God'. Very often the spiritual experience is one of awe, a sense of the presence of otherness. This deceives the recipient into thinking he is on a legitimate spiritual path and, therefore, right with God. I have often observed that false conversion is the outcome of religious awe.

Feeling 'the beat'

Recently I visited a large church where almost everyone was over forty. There was a rock and roll band with a lead singer and back-up vocalists. It was like the old days when we listened to hippie music in San Francisco's Golden Gate Park. For a full hour the band played mellow rock tunes with lyrics derived from the Bible. I enjoyed it very much — it was probably the 'best show in town' — and I stayed for the whole service. The service had a hypnotic effect and people were drawn to it. However, there was no gospel presentation and Jesus and the cross were hardly mentioned. At the conclusion, there was a short and perfunctory invitation for people to come forward for prayer.

The music and informality of the service were very attractive, but the people were being presented a Jesus with whom they could identify, not the Jesus who would bring them salvation. The service made people feel so good that they would surely want to come back just to feel the beat.

Spiritual counterfeits

There are those who exercise 'charismatic gifts', either in

private or in church, and they may be convinced that this means they have a saving relationship with Jesus. They may prophesy, speak in tongues, have a healing touch, receive a word of knowledge or have visions that come true, but having such gifts is not an indication of true conversion. Some people who are in cults that deny the deity of Jesus and reject orthodox Christian theology may display similar 'gifts'. Satan counterfeits genuine spiritual gifts and bestows them on those who deny Jesus. It is also true that some people can mimic genuine spiritual gifts (as any Pentecostal or charismatic minister can testify).

Healing is one of the genuine spiritual gifts (1 Cor. 12:9). Certainly there are many evidences throughout history and into our day of God miraculously bringing healing. Some people are fascinated with healing, while others, as a result of prolonged pain and the fear of death, are desperate for it.

Yet healing can be problematic. For instance, 'the healing touch' is practiced both in Christian circles and in occult groups. These people think they can control 'healing energies' by the movements of their hands. Such an experience may be seen as spiritual by the healer and the person healed, but when physical healing alone is the goal it can blind a person to their deeper need of conversion.

'Good times in the Lord'

In recent years there has been an emphasis on celebration and having 'good times in the Lord'. I have had these good times myself and although I do not look for them, I appreciate them when they come. Too often, however, good times in the Lord become the goal rather than a relationship with Jesus. Those who exclusively seek the good times are open to deception because they tend to see God as an indulgent parent who just wants everyone to be happy. Their view of God is not scriptural. When they are not celebrating or worshipping the God of the Bible, they are creating an idol for themselves. Behind the idol is the devil (1 Cor. 10:18–20). Satan is quick to exploit error, even in the midst of a celebrating congregation.

Celebrating in worship and having a good time in the Lord are fine, but they are no substitute for conversion. Without straightforward gospel preaching and a clear call to come to Jesus for salvation, joyous celebrants may be deceived into thinking they are Christians when they are actually unconverted. A converted person who celebrates and rejoices in the Lord with all his might will be pleasing to God. The unconverted cannot please God at all, despite the energy of their celebration.

The experiences of true and false conversions are varied, and yet on some points appear quite similar. As you examine your own heart in light of all these nuances, it is important to remember that if you discover you have just been 'playing at church', following a form of religion, or any such thing, the simplicity of Paul's answer to the Philippian jailer remains: 'Believe in the Lord Jesus, and you will be saved.'

10

SIGNS OF THE UNCONVERTED

We are all converts whether we practice an actual religion or spiritual discipline or not. In one sense then, the title of this chapter is inaccurate. Even the most ardent atheist is a convert — he is an adherent to his philosophical system. No one is a completely isolated, unaffected individual, free from any and all influences. Even the most 'free-thinking' nihilist is a convert.

There are characteristics or signs of the unconverted. These include the concepts they believe or disavow and the actions they value or reject. There are no surveys or studies cited in this chapter, rather, I am depending upon my many years of experience in active, public ministry and the testimony of Scripture. My purpose is to show that the unconverted — whether they are religious or not — have certain things in common and follow general thought and

behaviour patterns. I will also show the things that distin-
guish the non-religious unconverted from the religious
unconverted.

THE NON-RELIGIOUS UNCONVERTED

The non-religious unconverted reject Christianity, or to
be more precise, they reject what they think Christianity
is. They reject all forms of the obvious religious teachings that they have heard — the cultural myths and ideas
they have heard about who Jesus is or what Christianity
is all about.

The jilted

Some non-religious unconverted people reject all religious
connections as a result of a bad church experience. It is guaranteed that anyone who goes to church at all will, sooner or
later, have a bad experience. After all, the church is made up
of redeemed sinners who are still struggling with sin and
battling their old habits and desires. The very first church,
the one at Jerusalem, had problems as well (see Acts 5:1–11;
6:1–7; 15:1–21).

Other people have had unpleasant experiences with
Christians they have met or worked with and have rejected
the message because of the messenger. I am afraid I am guilty
here. There have been times when I was less than Christian
in my behaviour. I have become frustrated and angry in front
of non-Christians and they probably thought: 'What kind of
a Christian is he? Obviously his religion is not working
and I don't want what he has.' Christians are not perfect,
certainly, but we are often held to the highest standard, Jesus
himself, and we pale in comparison. Though we do not
always represent Jesus as we ought, still the integrity is there
because Jesus is wholly trustworthy.

Some people reject all forms of religion because of a bad
experience in a cult. It could be a religious cult, or a political,

commercial or educational/psychotherapeutic cult. There are thousands of cults in the world and they tend to quickly chew up their adherents and spit them out. Tens of thousands of people quit or are expelled from cults every year. Any pure and idealistic hopes that a former cult member might have held about Christianity may be severely damaged or destroyed. Consequently they might develop anti-religious attitudes towards all groups and religions.

The careerist

Excessive commitment to a career, or to a subculture connected with a job, may be a barrier to faith in Jesus. For example, a biology teacher turned away from his early Christian upbringing while he was in graduate school. There, professors and students alike scorned the slightest vestige of religiosity.

The careerist may also be so identified with his role that he will conform to the unspoken, but influential, philosophical outlook of his peer group. And, in some cases, being agnostic seems built into the vocation.

The key element here is peer pressure. Fitting in, being 'one of the gang', may be the difference between success and failure. Almost anyone could fall into this trap. Sometimes it literally comes down to whether you will identify yourself with Jesus and pursue a spiritual path, or be rejected and ill treated. Following Jesus requires courage.

A line from a song I learned long ago speaks to the issue: 'And when you found out where your heart should be, don't let the people say you've gone too far.' A certain amount of spirituality is okay but unconverted people have their limits, some quite narrow ones at that. They will express their strong opposition if you hold to Christian principles and this can be quite intimidating.

The hedonist

Some people reject biblical Christianity because they are satisfied with pursuing a lifestyle that they quite reasonably sense is outside the bounds of most religious moral principles. Really, they are forced to reject a spiritual teaching that focuses on moral values. Some of these people do embrace quasi-religious disciplines that have superficial but no moral content — of which there are many. These people tend to fear the light of the gospel and desperately search for reasons to retain and defend their sin.

Many years may pass before a hedonist comes to the end of finding pleasure in the lifestyle they have pursued. Satiated, cynical, and often guilt ridden, perhaps addicted to various substances, life seems cold and empty. Sometimes it is only then that they will consider the claims of Christ and be attracted to Jesus — just as many such people during the days of Jesus' earthly ministry.

The Gnostic

For the Gnostic, whether ancient or modern, there is a major disconnect between the mind and the body, between right and wrong. Being pure in thought and understanding the 'secrets of the ages', Gnostics believe they have freedom then to indulge in the lust of the flesh. The mind, the soul — these are the realms where the spirit operates. The flesh, the body — well, anything goes.

Gnosticism tends to be elitist, reserved for those 'in the know' and therefore, oddly enough, acceptable. Having right knowledge, initiated into the hidden mysteries, gives them licence to do as they please. This generally boils down to immoral behaviour. There was little moral restraint among the Graeco-Roman practitioners as history illustrates; it is different for the modern-day Gnostic where most cultures still do not readily approve open indulgence, especially of a sexual nature. The devout Gnostic is infuriated by such restraint and vehemently opposes any source of ethical teaching — and the most obvious offender here is Christianity.

The technocrat

There are also the stoutly non-religious technocrats who reject Christianity and place their hope in 'cyber salvation'. Amazing as it may seem, there are those who think technology — medical, computer or genetic — will be their salvation. Advances in medicine promise longer lives, perhaps even doubling the present life span. Some mistakenly suppose that by delaying death they can avoid it altogether. Cryonics, the freezing of a dead and diseased human in anticipation of restoring the body to life some time in the future when a cure for the disease has been developed, holds hope for some people. Some physicists and other cybernetic specialists envisage computer wizardry developing the possibility of immortality. Out there, somehow, a benign computer will clone or replicate people who will never die. There are biotechnologists who hope the 'death gene' can be blocked, thus preventing or slowing down the ageing process. Nanotechnicians envision tiny, micro-robots that will be able to repair or replicate worn out systems in the body.

Technocrats often explain their views in a quasi-religious fashion. Technocratic faith is non-spiritual; it is a religion without a transcendent God. It is new, exciting and 'scientific'. A growing number of people are attracted to it.

Akin to the technocrat is the person who, like myself before my conversion to Christ, hopes that creatures from an advanced civilization will arrive by spaceship and teach humans how to overcome disease and death. Science fiction writers have aided and abetted this idea. Fearing ridicule, I kept such thoughts to myself but UFO fans have achieved a degree of acceptance now so that the idea of rescue from beyond is no longer a strange and uncommonly held hope.

The existentialist

Perhaps the people who are most immune to true conversion are existentialists. They believe in their unique position as self-determining agents responsible for the authenticity of their choices. They are dedicated agnostics or atheists. They believe death is the end and life is to be a 'living in the moment'. It is somewhat akin to Zen Buddhism, without the formality or religious trappings. Meaning (or a justification for being) is found in honesty and integrity informed by cultural standards.

For existentialists to believe the grave is the absolute end requires faith — they cannot prove it. The resurrection cannot be proved either, in scientific terms, though there are compelling reasons to believe Jesus did rise from the grave. If physical death ends everything, what is done in the body now has limited consequences. And if the consequences of bad behaviour can be borne they say let us 'eat, drink and be merry for tomorrow we die'. This stream of thinking is quite convenient and alluring and existentialism continues to have a steady stream of 'converts'.

The humanist

Humanists are 'good people' who value their ability to reason, and believe that science will ultimately solve human problems. For them, meaning in life is found in fulfilling practical human needs. And, like the existentialist, the grave is the end — there is no heaven or hell.

A humanist who is also an activist — that is, someone who puts their money and energy where their head is — will generally find a significant degree of personal satisfaction in helping others and will gain recognition and respect. Thus affirmed the humanist is confirmed in his or her limited and incomplete view of life, a view that dismisses the claims of the Scripture as mythical.

The secular ethicist

There are 'ethical' atheists who earn advanced educational degrees and write learned philosophical papers about ethics. They value the classical virtues, espouse the timeless moral principles and endlessly argue the minutiae of ethical problems. They have no God who sets moral values however; rather, in their view, everything is relative.

The secular ethicist may believe in a god of some kind, one he feels comfortable with, but not a God who would judge anyone. It is enough to contemplate gods and goddesses who have nothing substantial to do with humans. They may have an academic respect for the ethical teachings found in the Bible but they reject Christianity.

The driven

There is a large group of people who are excessively occupied with their careers, families, friends or hobbies. (This category differs from 'the careerist' above.) They are hoping that the substance of life is in the daily process of getting things done. Often they are driven in their search for peace and security. Religion is something for which they simply have no time: it is irrelevant, something they do not need. Their focus is on the here and now. They forget that 'Man shall not live by bread alone' and that death will inevitably follow life.

Jesus told a story about a man like this. He had succeeded in business and needed to build larger and larger barns to store his crops. He said to himself, 'Take life easy; eat, drink and be merry' (Luke 12:19). That night he died and the question came, 'Then who will get what you have prepared for yourself?' (Luke 12:20).

Sometimes people in 12-step programmes like Alcoholics Anonymous (an addiction recovery group) can fall into this way of thinking. They can become driven by the needs of this life and take little thought for eternity. Freedom from addiction becomes their supreme goal and everything in their life becomes focused on the here and now. Overcoming addictive behaviour is worthwhile but it can also be all-consuming; we must remember that dying free of addictions does not merit any favour with God.

The do-gooder

During the middle years of life people often begin to search for meaning because they realize their time is running out. In evaluating their lives, they may conclude that they do not count for much. This may stir them to become enamoured with a cause — political, social, environmental — into which they can throw themselves. In this way, some measure of inner peace may be attained, but without God. Although good things may be accomplished (important and worthwhile things), there is no true peace without God and the great questions of life remain unanswered.

The old and cynical

In the twilight years, the unfulfilled and unconverted may become cynical. They give up. They become preoccupied with their bodily limitations and ailments. Since they have ignored and rejected Jesus all their lives, they will almost certainly end their lives the same way. Very few persons are converted late in life. I have seen this throughout my ministry. They know death is coming and they fear it. Most desperately hope that the grave is the end. Some, however, are stirred to search for true peace with God as deep in their being they remember a Sunday school class, or the testimony of a grandparent or parent, or the lines of an old hymn — something that refuses to let them be. If that is so, there is still hope, but it is dim.

THE RELIGIOUS UNCONVERTED

We live in a religious world. However, most 'religious' and 'spiritual' people are unconverted. These people are dear to my heart because they so often are sincere seekers of God but have been distracted or deceived.

There are two sub-divisions of the religious unconverted: the religious 'Christian' unconverted and the religious 'spiritual' unconverted.

1. The religious 'Christian' unconverted

The 'loving and fair-minded' liberal

The 'loving and fair-minded' liberal evaluates God based on his or her own sense of fairness; that is, a God who would judge and condemn a person is not deemed fair. It is assumed that God must be like us, with our immature sense of fairness. The God of Scripture is judged and found wanting. It is like the pot saying to the potter, 'What is the matter with you?'

This person is often a church member, even a leader or a minister. He rejects a God who would assign anyone to hell (if there is such a place), and espouses a God who is a 'loving heavenly Father' who will reward sincere people who try hard to do good. Passages in the Bible that speak of hell, judgement and condemnation are rejected, ignored or rein-terpreted. He believes that God accepts Gnostics, Hindus, Buddhists, Muslims, and so on, as long as they are good people — and probably even if they are not. Sin (if it exists) is no obstacle to admittance into heaven.

Genuine Christians may be bothered by the biblical doctrine of judgement and hell. No one relishes the idea that people will go to hell. I have struggled with this doctrine over the years but I retain it because I know it is solidly biblical and consistent with the holiness of God. It is not for me to judge God on the basis of my own sense of fairness.

The language and biblically-based terminology that most born-again Christians use, will sound funny, even ludicrous or ridiculous, to the liberal 'Christian'. To them the terms 'born again', 'saved', 'Lord Jesus Christ', 'second coming', and many others, do not have the sweet, lovely sound as they do to genuine Christians. Every Christian I have ever known loves to hear the simple message of Jesus and his cross preached. It is not so with loving and fair-minded liberals; such preaching will even be despised. The contrast here is remarkable, and is a clear sign that the spiritual/religious person has no real peace with God.

I have found that unconverted ministers and other sincere unconverted 'Christians' are particularly attracted to a God who is 'loving and fair-minded'. This concept of fairness as applied to God helps to reduce their anxiety about their own relationship with God, and the preaching of such a God is usually warmly received by the 'Christian' unconverted.

The 'loving' liberal has created an idol. Scripture has very little, if any, authority for him; therefore, he breaks the second commandment (Exod. 20:4–6). Only the God and Father of our Lord Jesus, who is a holy and righteous God, can cleanse and save us. The person who creates an idol cannot be converted by believing in and worshipping that idol. This misguided and undiscriminating notion of the love of God is surely a sign of the unconverted.

The mimic

There are those who have learned to imitate things Christian. I have met them in both charismatic and non-charismatic churches. It is easier to imitate Christian behaviour in charismatic churches because there is such a large emphasis on energetic activity in the church service.

A spectator can copy what he sees — e.g. raising of hands, singing in the Spirit, falling down 'under the power', dancing, shouting, speaking in tongues, reciting words of praise and worship — all of these things are quite easily done.

When a person does the right things and says the right things, other people are likely to believe he is a genuinely born-again Christian. Imitation happens in non-charismatic churches as well. When a person knows the right doctrines, knows the Bible well, knows the hymns — this person is fairly convincing. The mimic does not realize he is simply playing church. He is only doing what he has always seen done in his church. As a result, he is not aware of his unconverted state. The mimic may have been baptized, may read the Bible and pray, may sing and shout, but there has been no true conversion.

Over the years I have known many mimics. They often do not realize that they are merely acting a role; they sincerely believe they are genuine Christians. How can one know? It boils down to whether a person loves Jesus or not and is depending on Jesus alone, his death on the cross, his perfect sacrifice for our sin, for forgiveness of sin and salvation.

We know when we love someone. It is quite clear. There are the longings, the desires, the thoughts, the actions, the communion, and the fellowship — all for one person. So it is with loving Jesus, trusting in Jesus. The analogy is not perfect but useful. As Paul wrote in 2 Corinthians 13:5: 'Examine yourselves to see whether you are in the faith; test yourselves. Do you not realize that Christ Jesus is in you — unless, of course, you fail the test?'

The 'positive' thinker

There are those who believe in a 'positive' Christianity. These people have mistaken positive thinking for true biblical faith. They are quick to point out what they refer to as 'negative confessions'. They would never 'give place to the devil'. Healing and wealth belong to the 'faithful'. Their doctrines are full of magical thinking. There is usually no real understanding of the gospel, but there is a great deal of 'faith'. They use a religious vocabulary that is nearly unintelligible to anyone outside their own circle. They are always 'blessed', even when other people in similar circumstances would admit to being depressed, or at least disappointed.

Positive thinkers are often disappointed when life goes wrong. Either God must be blamed for misfortunes, maybe a church or they themselves for not being positive enough. These will 'feel' close to God when things are going well but depressed when they are not.

Those seeking a better quality of life

Some people are hoping to have their lives enhanced by religion. The church-growth movement targets these people quite successfully. 'Seeker churches', especially those attempting to start a new work, will send out slick brochures promising everything a person could hope for. They have activities for everyone, for all ages, for every situation: 'Come on down to the ... Community Church!' Leaders of these churches may be hoping to reach people and see them converted, but in the rush to fill the pews, a person's genuine conversion is not their prime concern. To get his life enhanced, the person seeking a better quality of life goes to a trendy church and adopts a Christian persona. He becomes Christianized, but he is not converted in most cases. Leaders of churches that cater to such people know that preaching a strong gospel is not the way to keep newcomers in the pews.

Those seeking a 'club'

Churches mean people — usually nice, friendly people — and the lonely are often attracted to them for no other reason than the company they offer. To attract new friends, a person may copy behaviour, conform and adopt a Christian persona, but never be converted. Often these people will end up in leadership positions in the church where they find companions, friends and recognition. They may become quite religious. They may teach Sunday school, join the choir and sit on boards and committees — all the while sleeping on the brink of hell. What pastor would challenge the conversion of these people? The answer is, unhappily, not many. To most, sadly, the day-by-day operation of their church is more important than the issue of heaven and hell.

Those bound by tradition

These are people who attend church for the sake of their parents, or to uphold their family's religious tradition, which tells them that if they do not go to church (at least once in a while) they are in deep trouble. They have a sense of conflict; they are driven by guilt. They may doubt, or even detest, the church or denomination in which they were brought up, but they are unable to make a break due to fear. They become Easter and Christmas 'Christians'.

Most commonly, people in this category belong to religious organizations that, according to the dogma of the church, hold the keys to heaven. What a terrible conflict this is! Emotionally and sentimentally there are strong ties to the church through their family bonds, but there is no real faith in God. Thoughts of leaving the church are distressing as there would be family or marital tension if they did so.

The superstitious

These are people who confuse magic and Christianity. They see God as a protection against bad things happening to them. It is much like childhood superstition. Right religious action, so they think, will bring good things, whereas neglect of religious duty or a sinful act (usually the fleshy ones involving sex or substance abuse) is bound to get them into serious trouble. Their slogan is 'What goes around, comes around.' This is magical thinking. They try to placate God so he will be good to them. This can become obsessive and result in extreme behavior. A person trying to stave off 'inevitable' punishment may look as if he is on the way to sainthood. These people are not converted; they have no peace; their sin is hanging over them like a monstrous cloud that rains despair into their lives. These religious but lost people, often very un-holy in secret, are insulated against the gospel. It is rare when such a person is converted.

The sentimentalist

There are so-called Christians who are enchanted with religious ritual and sentimental stories. They will become religiously 'inspired' about a story featuring a lost puppy and his guardian angel. Services with candles and a distant choir give them a warm glow. These are some of the sweetest people I know. They are caring and giving people who are willing to serve, but they are blind to the gospel. They have no worries as long as life is easy, but when trouble arises they have no peace with God to sustain them.

The serious seeker

Finally, there are the serious seekers after Jesus. These are people who read the Bible but cannot understand it; they have trouble comprehending the most basic concepts. They are often so uncomfortable in a worship service that I am surprised they attend at all. They occasionally reveal their discomfort by making noises, dropping hymn-books, rushing out to the toilet, checking on the children and doing other, even more disturbing things. I am most sensitive to these people. I think they are fighting against God as he shows them their sin and their need of Jesus. In fact, it is just these people that are most likely to be truly converted.

No doubt I too looked uncomfortable to Pastor Bob Lewis as he preached the gospel at the church where I was converted. What an unpleasant experience that was for me! When God is calling out and drawing us to Jesus, the mystery of conversion is unfolding right then and there. It is an awesome and unsettling event.

2. The religious 'spiritual' unconverted

In this group are some of my favorite people, but they tend to cause me a lot of frustration. They are so mellow and spiritual — often more than I am! They know that a spiritual life is vital to a healthy and satisfying life.

Inasmuch as alternative spirituality is their quest, they often dismiss anything to do with Christianity. Going to church for an hour seems unbearable, but they will sit on a hard floor to meditate for hours. Some of these people might submit to fantastic notions involving space aliens, abductions, teleportations and other phenomena, but they think a Christian miracle such as the virgin birth is impossible. Strangely, they often have a high regard for Jesus, yet they divest him of his true identity so that only an 'acceptable' caricature remains in their belief system.

To the religious spiritual unconverted, 'all paths lead up the same mountain.' They are attracted to Westernized versions of Eastern religions that promise a quick route to enlightenment, or a better reincarnation the next time around.

Alternative spiritual paths are attractive to those who desire something other than the normal fare. They may feel a sense of special power and uniqueness. Some enjoy having personal 'spirit guides' that channel their 'wisdom' to mere earthlings. To these people, communing with spirits is very enticing. They are blind to the counterfeits of Satan and naïvely accept anything that is 'spiritual'. For them,

Jesus is packaged in acceptable wraps, twisted and folded to fit whatever system of thought they may be engaged in (the system generally changes from time to time). It may be astrology, the Course in Miracles; then it might be yoga, or Zen. They are excited about whatever happens to be the latest trend: 'Have you heard about the new group that is working on past lives?' 'Have you been to the new psychic who is channelling Moses?' The marketplace of ideas is crowded and the aisles are full.

To make matters worse, some liberal 'Christian' ministers approve of almost anything that is 'spiritual'. They also believe that there are many paths to the top of the mountain. This is one of the most pernicious lies around today.

These unconverted people, wandering in the spiritual marketplace, will sometimes come to Jesus and be converted. They are seekers who are looking in wrong, even dangerous places. But once in a while, some of them will find Jesus, who is 'the way and the truth and the life' (John 14:6).

11

THE STAGES OF CONVERSION

A TRADITIONAL MODEL FROM THE FIRST GREAT AWAKENING

The great preachers of the eighteenth-century awakenings — Jonathan Edwards, Gilbert Tennant, Jonathan Dickinson, John Wesley, George Whitefield, Samuel Davies and many others — have greatly inspired me. This chapter is a discussion and summary of a sermon written by one of these, Jonathan Dickinson, to which he gave the title 'The theology of new birth'. It was written in 1741 and preached at the Presbyterian Church of Elizabethtown, New Jersey at the height of the First Great Awakening in America. Dickinson, one of the foremost Puritan preachers and first president of Princeton University, described the general process of conversion as it was understood by the moderate Calvinists of his day.

The full text of 'The theology of new birth' is given in Appendix I.§

The reason for focusing attention on these stages of conversion is that it takes us behind the standard evangelical model and the means developed by Charles Finney and those who followed after him. These stages more closely resemble the historic evangelical view of conversion held by the Reformers of the sixteenth century and those before them. In my view, these stages more accurately reflect the theology of conversion that is found in Scripture than anything developed in more recent times. Some of the material covered in this chapter is repetitive of that dealt with elsewhere in this book, but as part of Dickinson's sermon they have been preserved to maintain the flow of thought.

1. FACE TO FACE WITH SIN

The Holy Spirit brings a person 'to realize his own miserable condition, and see it as it is'. Jesus states that 'when he [the Holy Spirit] comes, he will convict the world of guilt in regard to sin and righteousness and judgement: in regard to sin, because men do not believe in me' (John 16:8–9). The unconverted person has an overriding interest in excusing himself and hiding from the truth. He fears coming to the light of God lest his sin be exposed. He fears the wrath and judgement of God (generally at an unconscious level), even though he may deny God's very existence. Conviction of sin must come from the One who really knows the sinner and has the authority to speak the truth. It is out of God's gracious love that he tells the sinner the truth — unforgiven sin will bring death and hell. The Holy Spirit must show the sinner his true condition because, as Paul wrote, 'As for you, you were dead in your transgressions and sins' (Eph. 2:1; see also Col. 2:13). The unconverted are blinded by sin

---

§ The headings for these stages have been supplied by the author.

and 'dead', unaware that they are lost. And, to make matters worse, 'The god of this age [Satan] has blinded the minds of unbelievers, so that they cannot see the light of the gospel of the glory of Christ, who is the image of God' (2 Cor. 4:4). The unbeliever's lost condition prevents him from seeing who Jesus is and what he did on the cross. It is no mystery to gospel preachers that 'the message of the cross is foolishness to those who are perishing' (1 Cor. 1:18).

I was once in such a state; I remember it well. I have seen it in others, hundreds of times. It is poignantly true that 'the man without the Spirit does not accept the things that come from the Spirit of God, for they are foolishness to him, and he cannot understand them, because they are spiritually discerned' (1 Cor. 2:14).

2. FACE TO FACE WITH HOPELESSNESS

The Spirit of God shows a person his utter inability to do anything about his condition. Dickinson uses the word 'humiliation' to describe the humbling of a man who supposes that by work and ingenuity a way can be found to avoid coming to Jesus for help. Dickinson states that in response to the experience of humiliation, many will struggle 'to establish their own righteousness, not submitting themselves to the righteousness of God'. The humiliation can be so strong that the unconverted person may believe he is unworthy of any mercy at all. He comes to the truth of Scripture: 'There is no one righteous, not even one' (Rom. 3:10). He will learn that 'all of us have become like one who is unclean, and all our righteous acts are like filthy rags...' (Isa. 64:6). He will see the truth that 'the heart is deceitful above all things and beyond cure. Who can understand it?' (Jer. 17:9). John Newton wrote: 'Amazing grace! How sweet the sound that saved a wretch like me!' He was amazed that God could love him since he knew God could see the rebellion in his heart. Eventually excuses and rationalizations cease; we cannot change ourselves.

We may stop one sin and replace it with another (such as pride) but any righteousness that is achieved apart from God, is short-lived.

The parable Jesus told of the tax collector and the Pharisee illustrates the hopelessness of attempting to appease God through good works. A tax collector and a Pharisee went simultaneously to the temple to pray. The Pharisee scorned the tax collector but judged himself to be righteous. As a careful observer of the law, the Pharisee kept the commandments and boasted to God. The tax collector, a Jew who had sold out to Rome and would have been hated and despised by his own people, could not even lift up his eyes to heaven, but beat his breast in a desperate demonstration of grief saying, 'God, have mercy on me, a sinner' (Luke 18:13). Commenting on the wretched tax collector, Jesus said, 'I tell you that this man, rather than the other, went home justified before God' (Luke 18:14).

We will either be like the Pharisee or the tax collector. To be like the tax collector we must see that we are lost and without remedy. This only comes from a revelation by the Holy Spirit of God.

3. FACE TO FACE WITH JESUS

The desperate sinner now develops an interest in Christ. Some of the Puritan preachers called this interest the pre-awakened state, which immediately precedes the awakened state of conversion.

At this stage the unconverted person realizes that 'salvation is found in no one else, for there is no other name under heaven given to men by which we must be saved' (Acts 4:12). This person has now come to the end of himself. It is to Jesus, and Jesus alone, that he looks. The issue must be settled. Will the sinner trust Jesus for his salvation and be converted, or will he walk away, perhaps for ever?

This is exactly what happened to me. I saw my sin; I realized that Jesus was the only Saviour, and I knew that if

I rejected him again, that might be my very last opportunity. That may not have been true, but that was how I felt.

It is the devil who is responsible for the idea that a person can make a decision to be converted and avoid hell any time he wants. The unconverted person must be enabled to come to Jesus by the Holy Spirit, and this only occurs when he comes into contact with the message of the gospel of Jesus, usually by preaching. Jesus states clearly, 'No one can come to me unless the Father who sent me draws him' (John 6:44). No one can see that Jesus is 'the way and the truth and the life' (John 14:6) except by the power of God.

The concept of a religious rite or quick prayer at a deathbed saving a dying sinner, no matter how afraid he might be of dying, has no biblical warrant whatsoever. There is the notable exception of the thief who was crucified alongside Jesus. God opened his heart and he heard Jesus say to him, 'Today you will be with me in paradise' (Luke 23:43). But last-minute conversion is exceptional and not to be relied upon.

4. FACE TO FACE WITH THE NEW BIRTH

The unconverted person now comes to Jesus and surrenders to him on his terms. This is the stage in which conversion occurs. And it happens in an instant.# A person may even be unaware that it has taken place. The testimony of someone who has prayed a version of the sinner's prayer often includes a memory of a particular moment in which he was 'converted' — whether he was truly converted then or not. However, true conversions are not always so well, or so easily, anchored to a particular moment in time. Some who are truly converted know it right away; others struggle for

---

Whether conversion is instantaneous or a process is an issue long debated. My view is that conversion, the actual spiritual birth, occurs in an instant, though it may not seem so to a person looking back on the experience. Conversion must also involve a process since there is always a story that goes along with it — conversion does not occur in a vacuum.

months, or even years, until they come to an assurance of salvation. It is more important that a person should *know* he is converted and safe in Jesus than to be able to identify the precise date and time when he prayed a prayer, or came forward in response to an invitation.

The unconverted person comes to Jesus without reservation, trusts in the sufficiency of Jesus and reaches out to Jesus, as one would grasp a strong tower in the midst of a raging storm. Here now is the mystery of conversion — this is the heart of it. Words are inadequate to describe what happens. It is a miracle that always leaves us dumbfounded. God the Father brings a person to the Saviour and enables that person to trust in Jesus. The gap, the abyss, is closed; God touches the finger of the torn and miserable creature and salvation is accomplished.

5. FACE TO FACE WITH GRACE

It is by grace that we are saved (Rom. 3:24; Eph. 2:8–9; Titus 2:11). Grace is God's undeserved favour. God reaches out to us, for no reason in ourselves, and offers forgiveness freely through the blood of his Son Jesus. Jesus died on the cross *in our place*, taking upon himself *our* sin and punishment, shedding his blood so that our sins are covered and the righteous demands of God's justice are fully satisfied. That is the meaning of grace. Faith, or trust, is the human response to God's grace. By faith we come to Jesus and receive God's grace. This, too, is a gift of God (Rom. 3:24).

By the power of God, all our sins are washed away in Christ. By the power of God, the sinner is regenerated, converted, born again (these three terms are synonymous) and is indwelt by the Spirit of God. That person's name is recorded permanently in the Lamb's book of life (Rev. 21:27).

After conversion, the Spirit of God carries on the work of grace in a believer's life — this is the process of sanctification. Sanctification is the setting aside of the believer for God's special service and work. The converted person now enjoys union with Christ (Rom. 6:5). He is able to abide in Christ, the Vine, and produce good fruit (John 15:5). The believer is *in* the world, but is not *of* the world (John 15:19; 17:14). The believer is perfect in Christ; however, he remains a sinner, so he is encouraged to confess his sin daily and to continue to rely on the blood and righteousness of Jesus (1 John 1:8–2:2).

In Jesus, we are sanctified and righteous (1 Cor. 1:30; 6:11). He is our holiness. There is no method of achieving sanctification; there is only resting in the righteousness and holiness of Jesus. Jesus said, 'I am the vine; you are the branches. If a man remains in me and I in him, he will bear much fruit; apart from me you can do nothing' (John 15:5).

Author's note: This sermon, in a paraphrased version, is useful to me when I do voluntary work at San Quentin Prison in the cell-to-cell ministry. It lends itself to a simple presentation, is easily understood and may be delivered adequately in five to ten minutes.

12

PROFILES OF TRUE AND FALSE CONVERSIONS

No two conversions are alike — whether true or false. In the case of true conversions, some people know the exact date and circumstances of their conversion, others have imprecise recollections.

Some people experience dramatic and instantaneous conversions. Others report a long process of conversion; they remember just a few clear landmark details. However, in every case, each converted person came to Jesus, often directly through prayer, for forgiveness and salvation.

The following profiles are based on my decades of experience as a pastor and minister. In each case I could only make an educated guess as to whether the person was truly converted or not. It is a delicate matter. I do not want to offend anyone, seem impertinent, judgemental or arrogant. Moreover, I do not want to confuse anyone either. But since the issue is so incredibly important, the only truly ultimate issue of life, I assume the risk for the purpose of providing some helpful examples to my readers.

For most of my ministry, I rarely asked people about how they became Christians. Now I do, not always, but often, and I listen carefully because my sole desire is that they be genuinely converted. I am not a judge; I am simply an ordinary sinner, but my hope is that all will be safe in Christ.

PROFILE OF A TRUE CONVERSION

X began to attend our Sunday morning worship service. He was always alone and did not bring a Bible to church. He would arrive late and leave early. I noticed that he was usually uncomfortable during the service, especially during the sermon. After four or five weeks of this, he phoned on a Monday morning and asked to speak with me in person, and we met later that day. He said that he had very little church experience as he had only been to church once or twice (but could not recall where or when). He became interested in church through watching Billy Graham on television and he had many questions regarding the exclusiveness of Jesus. He was concerned about all those people in the world who did not know of Jesus, and he also wanted to know if I believed in a literal hell — the usual questions.

It was quite clear from the beginning that he knew he was not a Christian. I asked if he understood his lost condition, and he said he did and this bothered him a great deal. We discussed what Jesus did on the cross and why he died there. He listened and asked thoughtful questions. At the end of the conversation, I urged him to come to Jesus for forgiveness and salvation. We prayed together. I prayed that God would show X his true condition and reveal Jesus to him. I asked X if he would like to pray with me for salvation, but he replied that he was not ready.

X did not show up at church for weeks. I was sure I had scared him away and I found myself wishing that I had been easier on him. (After all these years I still sometimes wish in hindsight that I had acted differently in a particular situation.) But several weeks later, X turned up and he was a different person. Right after the service he approached me and asked to speak with me. He told me he had decided to go to a number of other churches to see if what I said was true. He did not find one pastor who would agree with me, yet he had no peace. He said he remembered my prayer and began trying to pray himself. He thought about Jesus dying on the cross. When he began to place his trust in Jesus, he had peace for the first time and felt he was forgiven. He wanted to tell me all about it.

This occurred some time ago and I have had the opportunity of seeing X grow. He was baptized some months after his conversion. He studies his Bible, comes to church regularly, prays, tries to witness and contributes to the work. He is at peace.

PROFILE OF A TRUE CONVERSION

Q made a 'decision' after hearing a child-evangelism presentation. It was explained that she had a black heart, but she could choose to have a white one. She, of course, wanted to have a white heart, so she prayed a simple little sinner's prayer to obtain one. Was she converted at this time? There is no way of knowing.

Intellectually, Q knew the gospel story. Her theology was sound. She consistently made healthy moral choices. But she always worried that she had not had a crisis conversion similar to other people. When I asked her to tell me the story of her conversion, she could only refer back to her experience with the child evangelists. I found she had no assurance of salvation. There was no sense of her having come to Jesus.

Perhaps as a result of our conversation, Q responded to an invitation to rededicate her life. In a follow-up session with her, it appeared to me that she was converted, and she said that she was now resting in the righteousness of Jesus. I think that Q was born again at that rededication — not as a child who chose to have a white heart. The signs of a Christian are now seen in her life. The danger, as I see it, is that she might have gone through life thinking that heaven was her secure destination without any confirmation other than her childhood experience.

PROFILE OF A FALSE CONVERSION

Y is very 'spiritual'. She loves to get carried away and 'fall out' in certain church services. Frequently she asks questions about simple theological issues, but she does not seem to understand key Bible doctrines. She listens to, and sends small amounts of money to, many outrageous radio and television preachers, and she reports many miracles of healing. She has avoided attending church for long periods. At other times she has fluttered from one church to another.

She is offended by the exclusiveness of the cross. She thinks that God is too loving for Jesus to be the *only* way. In her own eyes, she is a spiritual, loving and caring person. She does not realize the danger she is in and will not even consider it. She is comfortable with religiosity and spiritual experiences. Although she claims to be born again, I believe Y has had a false conversion because she has no concept of coming to Jesus for salvation.

PROFILE OF A FALSE CONVERSION

Z is an accomplished Bible student who floats from church to church looking for someone to teach. He is entertaining and likeable; many are attracted to his charismatic personality.

In a lengthy conversation I had with him after church one Sunday it became evident that he had no conversion testimony. By that I mean he cannot state that Jesus is his Saviour. Strange that he could not because he knows his Bible so well. And he lives a clean and moral life. He regularly comes to church early and stays late. He is friendly, outgoing, helpful — all this and more. He is convinced that he is right with God, yet he is very uncomfortable when it comes to Jesus, his cross and our need to trust him alone for salvation. It appears that he is relying on his apparently upstanding moral behaviour and believing right doctrine. Z is a wonderful, 'spiritual' person, but in great danger.

PROFILE OF A FALSE CONVERSION

W was part of a 12-step programme that motivated him to seek out and develop a relationship with God 'as he understood him'. It was a hopeful beginning. We talked often of spiritual things — these were solid conversations, one after another — and it seemed to me that W was a genuine seeker after God. He came to church for months, but I knew he was not converted since Jesus meant little to him. Then he stopped attending church, stopped calling and stopped coming over to talk. I rang him to find out what was going on and he said he had found a new church, a more 'spiritual' church that respected all the world's religions.

W had been converted all right — but not to Christ! Now he knew that Jesus was saying the same as Buddha, Mohammed, Moses, Krishna and all the rest! He had 'it' now and he was happy. He was even going to start teaching a Sunday school class. He still wanted to be friends with me, but this 'Jesus thing' was too much for him. He invited me to his church, a mind-science, Gnostic, New Age group that even uses church-growth techniques to attract new members. I know of the group because I have received some of their brochures in the mail. It is a cult that hides its name and history while hoping to cash in on the current trend of spirituality. Many people are joining and it is becoming the fastest growing 'church' in the area.

W had experienced a false conversion. All I can do now is pray that the Holy Spirit will reveal Jesus to him before it is too late.

PROFILE OF A FALSE CONVERSION

At one time B had been a Jehovah's Witness, but she had rejected that. She was convinced salvation was based on knowledge and service. She was so energetic. She was willing to take on any task in the church. She was great to have around — she would work, work, work; she studied as though it was a full-time job — she could not get enough of the Bible. Most people were very impressed.

Early on I asked B how she became a Christian, but she could not say. She came out of the Jehovah's Witnesses, but not because she wanted Jesus. B was a religion-oriented person; the Bible fascinated her. She was able to win approval from people in the church because of her exceptionally hard work; she was busy earning her own righteousness. When I tried to explain true conversion to her, she could not accept God's grace — her refuge was her good works.

I let her go on working, and I even baptized her. What a mistake that was! Although I hoped her baptism might result in something wonderful, it did no good at all. It only helped to shield her from her lost condition. She figured that people who are born again are baptized, so she was baptized. After a short time, she wanted to be baptized again. When I baulked at that, she went to another church and was baptized again. Eventually she went to a number of churches who all baptized her and put her to work. She will probably remain in a church that does not challenge her relationship with God. I think she will one day return to the Jehovah's Witnesses.

PROFILE OF A FALSE CONVERSION

C was a convict at San Quentin State Prison. In his mid-thirties, he already had quite a long criminal record. He was now going to be serving a lengthy sentence.

C appeared to be sincerely full of remorse. For weeks after arriving at the prison, he was almost overcome by what had befallen him. There were tears and more tears. He professed that he would never use drugs or hurt anyone again — ever. He found comfort at the chapel because he was unconditionally accepted by the convicts and volunteers working there — volunteers like myself.

One evening I had a chance to talk with C at length. By now he was over the shock of being back in prison; as every convict must, he had come to terms with the inevitable. We spoke of his life and the tragedy that it was. He did not understand that he had sinned against a holy and righteous God. He did not see that when he committed his crimes he was directly transgressing God's just laws. C was full of remorse, but his biggest regret was that he had been caught. He was not repentant because he did not see that he had sinned against God. C was not converted but he had learned to be very religious — so religious that he was fast becoming a leader at the chapel. It was no wonder he had convinced himself and those around him that he was a born-again Christian. Yet he had no conversion testimony. He had not been to Jesus for cleansing from his sin, though he thought highly of Jesus and said that he loved him. C had not come to Jesus as Saviour although he called him 'Saviour'.

Is this too harsh a judgement? Maybe. Nevertheless, I believe that a Christian will be clear about his need for forgiveness. There must be some testimony, however minimal. C had learned to parrot the preachers, but when I questioned him closely, it was readily apparent that he had no conversion testimony.

PROFILE OF A FALSE CONVERSION

D was a happy member of a family-oriented church, a fine church with an attractive building and activities for people of all ages. He and his family were very much involved in the life of their church. D was given some tapes of my sermons on conversion, and they upset him greatly. He was a Christian, he told me, but he had never heard such long and strange sermons.

During a phone call (we never did speak face to face) I plainly told him that I liked him but that he was not converted. (In those days, I rarely had the courage to actually say such a thing!) But this was not a difficult judgement to make. He had no testimony that his sins were forgiven. He had no appreciation of Jesus as his Saviour. This is an example of Christianization and not true conversion. In fact, D had no idea that he *needed* to be converted. D is a likeable and sincere person who is sleeping soundly on the brink of hell. He rejected what I was saying and got the minister of his church to agree with him. That, so far, is the end of it.

PROFILE OF A TRUE CONVERSION

During the course of the writing of this book I discussed its central themes with another pastor. I noticed that he questioned me quite closely on several points. Although he had been preaching the gospel for many years, he had not carefully considered the nature of true conversion. He preached the gospel, used the traditional invitation and relied on the sinner's prayer.

After a meeting one evening he confessed that he had been angry with me for questioning the very practices that he had been committed to for so long. He said it rattled him to a considerable degree to have to evaluate the basic premise of his entire ministry. He even had to evaluate his own conversion — a startling event indeed! However, his examination yielded an assurance of salvation and a fresh start for his ministry. He saw clearly that the most important element of his life's work was that the people in his church were actually converted and going to heaven.

PROFILE OF A FALSE CONVERSION

N is a 'people' person, gregarious, loves small groups (where bonding is the chief goal), is a real pleasure to visit with and is familiar with a number of contemporary spiritual practices. She considers herself a 'healer', and relies on quasi-occult practices like the 'healing touch' to bring health and comfort to those in need. It is reported that she has brought healing and relief to a number of people and she has gained some notoriety as a result.

N claims to have been a Christian for as long as she can remember. Her father and her mother had been ministers for a time with the Unitarian Church, but she, unlike them believes in the Trinity. She believes Jesus in the only way to God because she reports that Jesus had appeared to her as a little girl and healed her when she was ill. Quite convincing.

To N, Jesus is the Great Physician, the great healer, and she says she uses Jesus' power to heal people. N considers herself to be orthodox theologically, too. But after many conversations it has become clear she is relying on her childhood 'vision' of Jesus and her subsequent healing as evidence of her Christianity. She does not like to hear biblical teaching and preaching but is more attracted to meditation groups where emotional and spiritual healing are the focus.

PROFILE OF A FALSE CONVERSION

F, raised in a Christian home, was taken to church three times a week by his parents. Baptized at an early age, he did not mind going to church so often, and to the best of his recollection, believed all the standard evangelical doctrines.

After graduation from college he left home for military service — and he left his Christianity behind.

I met F at a wedding reception and we got off to one side of the large hall and began a rather animated discussion. Close in age, we talked together like we were old friends. He knew many of the same Bible verses and hymns I did. After a short time I realized F was not a Christian at all; my ear picked up phrases and ideas common to the 'American' Buddhists I knew. When F talked about being 'present in time' and 'really living each day' my suspicions were confirmed.

F had been meditating for almost thirty years and was a committed Buddhist. He did not bristle when I suggested that he had never become a Christian in the first place but had merely been Christianized. I carefully explained what that meant, and F agreed with me quite emphatically. He did, however, believe that his parents had been genuine Christians. But since F believed that 'truth was relative', he was sure that both he and his parents were essentially on the same track, just different sides of the mountain.

PROFILE OF A TRUE CONVERSION

T was born and raised in a Bible-based cult that does not hold to historic orthodox Christian doctrine but is anti-trinitarian and considers itself to be the only true 'church'. T, however, read the Bible as a college student and in a clear and definite way discovered that Jesus had saved him. It was shocking and dangerous all at once. As time went on he found others who had also become real Christians but who could not, due to their families, leave the 'church' for a more orthodox Christian group.

T had to live the life of an underground Christian even while living in America! Through the internet he connected with a Bible study and prayer group and was following Jesus as Lord. He had hopes of one day moving to another state and being able to openly proclaim himself a Christian.

13

ASSURANCE OF SALVATION

There is good reason for Christians to examine themselves to be sure they are truly converted. The Apostle Paul encourages the Corinthians: 'Examine yourselves to see whether you are in the faith; test yourselves. Do you not realize that Jesus Christ is in you — unless, of course, you fail the test?' (2 Cor. 13:5). There must not be any surprises on the Day of Judgement. By examining ourselves to see if Jesus Christ is in us we will come to an assurance of our salvation.

PERSONAL EXAMINATION

There have been a number of times in my own life when I have had to examine myself to see whether I was 'in Christ'. My personal insecurity, the accusations of the enemy, my failure to control fleshly desires — these and other things brought me to my knees, looking to God for comfort and assurance. This is a normal and necessary part of the Christian life; we all go through these times.

Having an assurance of salvation is essential to a healthy Christian life. Without assurance of salvation, a believer's spiritual growth will be stunted. Coming to assurance of salvation is a normal process, both for those who have a precise memory of their conversion and for those who do not. People who experience a dramatic conversion may subsequently doubt their salvation. Others, who are not aware of the time of their conversion because they were raised by godly parents and think they have belonged to Jesus from a very early age, may also struggle with assurance. The circumstances of conversion are not central: whether a person can point to a definite conversion date or not matters little in arriving at assurance.

Indeed, coming to an assurance of salvation is, in some measure, a subjective and personal experience. Therefore, truly converted people may doubt their conversion at some point in their lives; in fact, most will lack assurance from time to time. It is doubtful that a non-Christian would even be worried about whether he was genuinely converted or not.

A person, then, may be genuinely converted and still have little or no assurance. Thus, he may attempt to earn forgiveness by doing good works. It was that way with me. As a new Christian, I kept struggling to 'be good'. At times I would feel that I was not good enough to be with all those upstanding people at church. My sin, though it may not have been evident on the surface, was ever before me. But my idea of the Christian life was erroneous: I did not realize that believers are still sinners who are wholly and completely covered by the blood of Jesus. I had started with faith but I was trying to continue by works. I had no assurance of salvation.

What things in a person's life cause them to be worried that they are not born again? A failure in ministry, such as being dismissed from a ministerial position, may seem to signal a cause for alarm. Moral failures, such as adultery, substance abuse, financial fraud or embezzlement, may seem to be proof that a true conversion could not have taken place. Doctrinal struggles (even lapses), becoming entrapped in a cult, personal misfortunes, serious illnesses, tragic deaths — any of these, and many others, may bring a person to question their salvation. However, a truly converted person will continue to trust Jesus in the midst of failure, confusion and discouragement and will *eventually* follow Jesus once more. The righteous person will stand again with Jesus even after taking a body blow, so to speak. The unconverted will not, they will fall away.

There are also objective evidences of conversion (see chapter 6). One of these signs of conversion is a change in attitude toward Jesus. Jesus may have been feared, despised, ignored, regarded as simply another great spiritual teacher, or prophet, as merely one of many founders of a religion, and so on; or his true nature — that of God in the flesh — may have been misrepresented. After true conversion, Jesus is seen as the resurrected and living Saviour, and the converted person is attracted to Jesus and begins to submit to him as Lord of their life.

Another sign of conversion is a desire to turn from sin and, in fact, an actual turning away from known sin. The commandments of God become guidelines for living. A love for the church and those who form a part of it begins to develop as we learn that we are commanded to love one another. One command in particular, that to be baptized, will be followed. A converted person will begin to identify with Jesus, will not deny his name and will be willing to suffer persecution on account of Jesus. Preaching of the gospel will be a pleasure to hear, whereas before it was convicting, unpleasant and often avoided at all costs. There will be a growing desire — indeed, a need — for Bible study and prayer. The converted person will have a longing to know God through his Word and talk with him in prayer.

Gratefulness for the forgiveness of sins is also a sign of conversion. In Luke 7:36–50 we read the story of a sinful woman who poured out her love and gratefulness to Jesus for the forgiveness he had given her. In a rather remarkable display of emotion, the woman, a notorious sinner, walked uninvited into the home of a Pharisee named Simon and proceeded to kiss the feet of Jesus, wash them with her tears and anoint them with costly perfume. Simon, along with the other guests, was astonished that Jesus would allow himself to be touched by a common sinner. But Jesus said: 'her many sins have been forgiven — for she loved much. But he who has been forgiven little loves little' (Luke 7:47). Her love and devotion was a measure of the gratefulness she had for Jesus because she knew her sins were forgiven. Jesus then went on to say to the woman, 'Your sins are forgiven' (Luke 7:48).

HAVING ASSURANCE

How does a person come to an assurance of salvation? I am unable to recall when or how I came to assurance. Furthermore, I am not so sure I 'came' to it at all. I believe God confirmed my salvation to me. I could not talk myself into assurance; it came little by little. God shows us our security in Jesus and we then rely on what God has revealed. That wonderful verse, Romans 8:16, states that 'the Spirit himself testifies with our spirit that we are God's children'.

Paul had come to an assurance of his salvation:

And of this gospel I was appointed a herald and an apostle and a teacher. That is why I am suffering as I am. Yet I am not ashamed, because I know whom I have believed, and am convinced that he is able to guard what I have entrusted to him for that day (2 Tim. 1:11–12).

Paul was not ashamed (fearful that he had erred) because he knew the power of God to save. Paul had confidence in

Jesus, not in himself. The verb 'have believed' is the perfect *active* indicative and means that the initial saving event had occurred in the past (in Paul's case, on the Damascus Road) and also that salvation was continuing and would continue indefinitely. The verb 'am convinced' is perfect *passive* indicative and means that Paul had been convinced of his salvation and did not come to assurance on his own. Paul's assurance was given to him.

There is an urgent need to come to an assurance of salvation. Let us examine the warning of Jesus in the Sermon on the Mount quoted earlier:

> Not everyone who says to me, 'Lord, Lord,' will enter the kingdom of heaven, but only he who does the will of my Father who is in heaven. Many will say to me on that day, 'Lord, Lord, did we not prophesy in your name, and in your name drive out demons and perform many miracles?' Then I will tell them plainly, 'I never knew you. Away from me, you evildoers' (Matt. 7:21–23).

It is obvious that some of those who will hear the fateful words, 'Away from me!' will be religious people. In fact, many of them will have been very religious indeed! The people about whom Jesus spoke had prophesied, cast out demons and performed miracles. This may describe some members of 'Christian' groups that feature powerful 'gifts'. Jesus' description may also apply to magicians and psychics who try to mimic the authentic gifts of the Holy Spirit. For example, Simon the magician tried to purchase the power of God so that he could do great miracles (Acts 8:9–25) and the seven sons of Sceva invoked the name of Jesus to drive out evil spirits (Acts 19:14–16).

I believe many people whom Jesus will tell on Judgement Day that he 'never knew' them will have been lost because of false conversions. This is indeed tragic. Read again those verses from Matthew 7. The miracle-workers thought they had a relationship with Jesus. They called Jesus 'Lord', but Jesus said he did not know them. Was this a case of false conversion? I say, 'Yes, theirs was a false conversion.' We must make sure that our conversion is genuine.

A DIFFICULT EXAMINATION

The question of whether they are saved is fearful for some people to consider. Those who most need to come to an assurance of salvation are often the most fearful of what they might discover. Fear is overcome by admitting it and by laying it at the foot of the cross. We must say, 'Lord, do you know me? Am I yours? I come to you now because I need to know that you have saved me and that my name is written in your book. I will not try to prove my salvation by reciting my virtue. I rely on you alone.'

In our sinful condition, coming to God can be a fearful thing. He is the great Judge, holy and righteous. We cannot even approach him. We come to him through the only mediator between God and man, Jesus the Messiah, who gave his life for us on the cross, who was raised from the dead and now sits at the right hand of the Father, interceding for us. Once we are assured of our salvation, we come to God boldly and confidently, in Jesus name.

Some, out of fear that they are not forgiven, attempt to earn forgiveness by doing good works. Others look for signs and wonders as proof of their conversion. They think that God must hold them in high favour if he grants them such miracles. Still others think they will find salvation in the Bible itself — through their knowledge of Scripture and their ability to quote the Bible in great detail. Paul said, 'Jews demand miraculous signs and Greeks look for wisdom, but we preach Christ crucified: a stumbling block to Jews and foolishness to Gentiles' (1 Cor. 1:22–23).

We have to deal with our fears; we also have to deal with our shame. Shame is something that we run and hide from; it is only natural that we do so. But it is better to experience shame now rather than on the Day of Judgement. Do you recall my story of the pastor who came forward in response to an invitation right in front of his own congregation? No doubt he fought back feelings of embarrassment and shame. But he realized that what others might think of him meant very little. He had his eyes on Jesus, not on those in the pews. Pastors, ministers or church members reading this book may realize their own unconverted state and see the ugly spectre of shame arising before them. What will you do? Will you hide, out of shame and fear, or will you ignore your shame and embarrassment and come to the cross and the Saviour?

Let each of us examine our own conversion. Whom are we trusting for forgiveness of sin and salvation? The following are all responses that I have heard from people when I asked them how they knew they were born-again Christians:

I try to do good.
I was baptized.
I have always gone to church.
I have always believed in God.
I have always prayed to God.
I was baptized in the Spirit.
My grandfather was a minister.
I am a spiritual person.
I made a commitment to Christ when I was young.
I have always loved God.
I went forward once in a church.
I prayed to accept Christ.
I used to go to church.
I went to Sunday School when I was little.
I have never hurt anybody.
I raised my hand in church.
I have stopped drinking and using drugs.
I read the Bible all the time.

Every one of these experiences is commendable. However, the question asked was how they knew they were Christians. There was no mention of their being lost, no mention of Jesus' blood, no cross, no resurrection — none at all. Each item in the list is a *work* and, you may rest assured, I pressed every person and gave them every opportunity to make clear what they meant. I did not put words in their mouths. I was not looking for the 'right' phrases. I challenge preachers of the gospel to try it for themselves. Ask people what they are relying on for their salvation. *Urge them to be rigorously honest about their condition*. Warn them about merely repeating statements of faith, which they think you are expecting to hear. Acknowledge the anxiety they may feel and thus the temptation to agree and conform. Find out for yourself.

I have had numerous opportunities to discuss my views on conversion with many pastors. To date, I have found few pastors who expressed concern about whether or not people in their churches were converted and assured of salvation. The rest realized the problems that might result from preaching conversion-oriented sermons. I was not shocked about their reluctance to preach for conversion and assurance of salvation because I felt the same way throughout most of my pastoral ministry.

To those who want to bring conversion to the lost and assurance of salvation to those who are unsure, here are some suggestions of questions to ask:

1. Describe how you became a Christian.
    a. Did you see a need to be forgiven?
    b. Did you see Jesus as the Saviour?
2. How do you now view Jesus?
3. What do you now rely on for forgiveness and salvation?
4. Do you have an assurance of your salvation?
5. What would you say to God on Judgement Day as to why you ought to be in heaven?

A strong assurance of salvation in Jesus is a wonderful thing, more precious than any possession. Recall the words of Jesus: 'Whoever comes to me I will never drive away' (John 6:37). Our relationship with God is strong and unbreakable because the strength belongs to Jesus, who will never drive us away.

In Jesus we are safe, we are secure. Not even our sin will cause Jesus to drive us away or release his firm hold on us. We shall be disciplined (Heb. 12:4–13); we shall be reproved (Rev. 3:19); but we shall never be rejected or abandoned (Heb. 13:5). Jesus calls us to obedience through his unchanging love; it is always love which moves us to faithfulness. Fear of rejection and the anxiety that stems from the demand to perform often leads to failure and despair. We must rest entirely on the person and finished work of our Lord Jesus Christ to experience the blessing of assurance of our salvation.

Let us come to an assurance of our salvation. Let us speak of it in our conversation, preach it, teach it.

14

JACOB BECOMES ISRAEL: A SYMBOL OF CONVERSION

Jacob wrestled with God and prevailed (Gen. 32:22–32). Therefore, God changed his name to Israel, which means 'He struggles, or wrestles, with God.' If Jacob had run away, if he had given up the fight, he would not have been 'converted'. He did not run; he wrestled with God all night.

I use this story of Jacob as a metaphor for conversion. Jacob wrestled with God as we wrestle with the work of the Holy Spirit who reveals both our sinful state and the remedy for the penalty of our sin. God's love and grace will triumph in the end.

My wrestling with God lasted about nine months. For the first time in my life, I was face to face with my sin and my need of a Saviour. It was intense and unpleasant. I could not get away from the convicting work of the Holy Spirit, although I did not understand the source of my discomfort.

When the unconverted person hears the gospel, he may wrestle with God. Some do so intensely, others much less so. There is a tendency on the part of Christians to comfort the unconverted person when he is in such pain; I think this is a mistake because that person is wrestling against the conviction of the Holy Spirit. We must not let the unconverted be comforted with anything less than the peace of forgiveness and the assurance of salvation. I have often made the pastoral mistake of comforting a person by giving him an unfounded affirmation of his 'Christianity'. Sometimes a person whom I had comforted later returned to me and told me about his conversion in a setting where he had wrestled with God. I wonder how many of those whom I have falsely comforted remain in their lost state.

Previously the psychological phenomenon of introjection was discussed. This occurs when an individual who is in a tense social situation acts (probably unconsciously) to reduce their anxiety. An unconverted person wrestling with God is in a state of discomfort. Such a person may not be able to be totally honest with himself. He may be tempted to agree with a Christian for no other reason than the unconscious desire to reduce anxiety.

The methods we employ to bring people to saving faith may instead provide false comfort and result in false conversions. The standard invitation and use of the sinner's prayer (almost sacred icons of evangelical Christianity) may do more to circumvent an unconverted person's wrestling with God than any device practiced today. Rigorous intellectual honesty and personal integrity must be observed on the part of both the unconverted person and the Christian witnessing if false conversion is to be avoided.

Invitations to come forward and recite a prayer to accept Jesus can be tricky at best, and dangerous at worst. When I reached the front of the auditorium at the First Baptist Church of Fairfield, California, I was shaking. A deacon met me there and sat me down on the first pew. I was scared.

There was no possibility of my disagreeing with, or even questioning, the deacon. No serious discussion was going to take place. It was a matter of extricating myself from the situation as quickly as possible. I wanted to please that deacon so much I could not be genuine about my feelings. I was in a submissive position, and I repeated verbatim every word of the sinner's prayer that he told me to pray. Thankfully, God did not leave me alone. He continued to wrestle with me and I eventually came to know him truly, through Christ.

For twenty-nine years of my pastoral ministry I knew what to do at the conclusion of a presentation of the gospel — I gave an invitation to come forward. I would then talk to the person and pray some version of the sinner's prayer with him or her. I no longer do this. That is not to say that I will never again give an invitation, or that I think it is absolutely wrong to do so. However, I now call on people to *come to Jesus* for forgiveness and salvation. I do not offer them a mechanism that would facilitate (much less guarantee) a true conversion.

I used to boast that if I had an hour to present the gospel to someone, that person would become a Christian. Frankly, I shudder at that now. Yes, an hour with a person who had somehow come to me, and the opportunity to persuade that person about Christ would nearly always result in a 'conversion'. Few people had the capacity to withstand my arguments, especially when it would have created an unpleasant situation if they refused to pray with me for salvation. Many of these were not converted, as subsequent experience sadly demonstrated, and I was not able to figure out why. Some who I 'converted' were not converted to Christ at all.

This way of urging people to come to Jesus is not easy for me to give up because I still want to personally affirm a person's conversion; I still want to report the number of conversions and add to the numbers in the pews. There is a part of me that would like to have the magic to convert, to control and to announce salvation. I struggle with those tendencies. However, I am not the mediator, Jesus is. I am not the priest, Jesus is. I am not sitting at the right hand of the Father in heaven, Jesus is. I am not 'the way and the truth and the life', Jesus is. As a preacher of the gospel, I bring people to Jesus, Jesus alone.

In place of my old practice of inviting people forward to recite the sinner's prayer, I urge them to come to Jesus in prayer and confess their sin, repent of their sin, trust Jesus and his blood to cleanse them of sin and acknowledge Jesus as their living, resurrected Lord and Messiah. I ask them to pray to Jesus where they are, whether seated or standing, and I may even invite them to come forward and kneel at the front of the church and pray. In addition, I invite people to speak with me after the service or to make an appointment to talk with me later in the week. At that time, I speak to them about coming to Jesus; I explain the objective aspects of conversion. I do not act as a priest standing between man and God; I point to Jesus and his cross.

The unconverted person who comes into significant contact with the message of Jesus may wrestle strenuously against God. A life-and-death struggle is being fought. The pastor or Christian who is witnessing must be very mindful of the seriousness of that war and the only weapons available — his love for the lost person, his prayers and the message of the gospel of Jesus Christ — to carry on his servant ministry (Eph. 6:10–20).

APPENDIX I: 'THE THEOLOGY OF NEW BIRTH'** BY JONATHAN DICKINSON

I am, then, to consider in what manner the Spirit of God quickens dead sinners and brings them into a state of spiritual life.

To this end I shall in general observe that the principal method by which this great change is wrought in the heart of a sinner by the Spirit of God is in giving him a realizing view of the great truths revealed in the Word of God, and enabling him to see things as they are. It may be some prejudice against the doctrine of our sanctification by the special influences of the Spirit of God upon our hearts, that

** This sermon was preached by Jonathan Dickinson (1688–1747) at Elizabethtown, New Jersey in 1741. The spelling, punctuation and other minor details of style have been slightly edited for the purpose of clarity to the modern reader. Scripture quotations have been left in the eighteenth-century version of the KJV to retain the flow of language.

men may imagine there is hereby intended the infusion of some new faculty into the soul which it had not before, and that the new creation implies our becoming a new sort of being, with respect to the natural powers and properties of the soul, which we were not before. But let it be considered that the Spirit of God does no more in the conversion of a sinner than bring him to the right exercise of those rational powers with which he was born, give him a just view of his greatest concerns and enable him to act worthy of a reasonable being. Observe this, and all the prejudices against the doctrine before us are obviated and vanish away.

Now that this is the case I shall endeavour to show it by taking some particular notice of the usual progressive steps by which a sinner is brought out of a state of carnal security to the possession and exercise of the divine life; and I think it will appear that the whole change is wrought in him by spiritual illumination, by impressing a right view of things upon his mind, or by enabling him to act reasonably.

1. Then, if we consider the first change wrought in a sinner by the Spirit of God, it will appear to be no more than his *bringing him to realize his own miserable condition, and see it as it is.* It is awfully certain from the Word of God that every impenitent sinner is an enemy to God, under a sentence of condemnation and an heir of hell and eternal misery.

And it is equally certain that most in the world are easy and quiet, careless and secure, in this dreadful state. No means that can possibly be used will put most of mankind upon a proper solicitude about their eternal welfare. The most awakening addresses that can be made them in the name of the Lord, the most surprising alarms of God's providence, the most pathetic and compassionate entreaties of their godly friends, have no effect upon them, to stop their career for hell and damnation. They will yet sleep upon the brink of the pit. ... They will yet indulge their lusts, though they perish for ever.

And what is the source of this indolence, thoughtlessness and security, but their want of a just view of their state and danger? Could they but realize these things, and see them as they are, they would sooner rush upon a drawn sword, or leap into a burning furnace than further incense the eternal Majesty against their souls and venture upon everlasting damnation. But their misery is that they have no feeling apprehension of these things. They consider them but as the rumbling of remote thunder, and as affairs of no special consequence to them; and thus they will consider them, unless the Spirit of God impresses this important concern upon their mind, and gives them a lively sense of what they are doing, and where they are going.

But if once the blessed Spirit undertakes the work, he will make the long-neglected and slighted means of grace effectual to open their eyes, that they may see their state as it is. Though they could before sit under the most powerful ministry from year to year, without care, fear, or sensible apprehension of their danger, yet now an ordinary sermon, or a particular passage in a sermon, which perhaps they had heard hundreds of times before without concern, shall awaken their sleepy consciences and make them with trembling and astonishment cry out, 'What shall I do to be saved?'

Why, what's the matter now? Whence is this wonderful change? Why can't the poor sinner do now as he used to do? Why can't he go on in his mirth and jolliness, in his worldly pursuits and sensual gratifications? What means this darkness and distress, this melancholy countenance and solemn concern? Is this the man that lately laughed at preciseness, that bantered serious godliness and ridiculed vital piety as 'enthusiasm', or a heated imagination? Why is he now as much an enthusiast as any of those whom he lately derided and scoffed at? Why is he now so afraid of hell and damnation, that could lately mock at fear, and laugh at the shaking of God's spear?

This wonderful alteration is wholly wrought by the almighty Spirit's impressing a lively view of what the secure sinner could have no feeling sense of before. Now he sees his sins, in their number, nature and aggravations. Now he sees his danger and thence feels that it is a fearful thing to fall into the hands of the living God. He sees it in such a view that he can no longer be quiet and easy in such a state of guilt and misery. But this (though open to everyone's observation and plainly visible from the Word of God and the nature of things) is what he never would have seen to purpose, unless the Comforter had been sent to convince him of sin. And the reason is assigned: 'The god of this world hath blinded the minds of them which believe not' (2 Cor. 4:4). And, 'Israel doth not know, my people doth not consider' (Isa. 1:3).

2. If we consider the case with respect to a sinner's *humiliation*, the Spirit of God works this also in the soul, by showing him his state as it is, and by giving him *a realizing sight of his unworthiness of divine mercy, of his spiritual impotency and utter inability to help himself.* These are indeed truths plainly revealed in Scripture, as well as necessary deductions from the light of nature. By both of these it is clearly manifest that we are guilty creatures, and thereby worthy of the wrath of God; that we are imperfect creatures, and therefore cannot fulfill the demands of the law of nature; much less can we make satisfaction for our past offences.

But, although these things are in themselves evident of the light, they have no impression upon the minds of the majority of mankind. Though deserving nothing but destruction and death, they are as easy and secure as though they had a title to God's favour and a claim to eternal happiness. Though utterly incapable to change their own hearts, or to deserve that God should do it for them, they are yet attempting their salvation in their own strength, if they attempt it at all, and 'being ignorant of God's righteousness, they go about to establish their own right-eousness, not submitting themselves to the righteousness of God' (Rom. 10:3).

Even those who are convinced of their guilt and danger are usually struggling for deliverance in their own strength, betaking themselves to some self-righteous refuge or other. And thus in their highest attainments will they continue to compass themselves about with sparks of their own kindling, until the Spirit of grace, by his power-ful influences, humble them at God's feet, and show them that they are 'wretched, and miserable, and poor, and blind, and naked' (Rev. 3:17).

And how is this done, but by giving them a sight of their case as it is? They had a *doctrinal* knowledge before, that they were sinful, guilty, helpless and hopeless in themselves. But this had no special influence upon their affections, or their conduct. But when they have a *feeling* sense of this, it must bring them low. They now see their sin and guilt, that there is no resting in their present condition. They see the defects of their duties, that these cannot recommend them to God's favour. They see their own impotency; that they cannot take away the heart of stone out of their flesh, and give themselves a heart of flesh. They see the strict demands of God's law; that it is impossible to come up to them. They see the purity and holiness of God's nature; that he cannot look upon sin and sinners with approbation. They see that they have no capacity to help themselves though they are utterly undone in their present condition.

And what is the necessary result of a realizing sight of such a lost, helpless, perishing condition, but that 'If thou, Lord, shouldest mark iniquities, O Lord, who shall stand?' (Ps. 130:3). Or that, 'Behold, we are before thee in our trespasses: for we cannot stand before thee because of this'? (Ezra 9:15). What should be the result of this prospect, but that they lie at God's footstool, as condemned malefactors, having nothing to plead, save unmerited and forfeited mercy, why sentence should not be executed upon them, to their eternal confusion?

3. In the same manner, a convinced sinner is brought to *a solicitous enquiry after an interest in Christ*. This also is wrought in him by a lively view of his case as it is. We are all indeed, from our earliest age, indoctrinated in this essential article of the Christian faith, that there is not salvation in any other but Christ, and that 'There is no other name under heaven and among men, whereby we must be saved' (Acts 4:12). And yet most of the world are 'whole, and need not the Physician' (Mark 2:17). They are more concerned about anything else than about an interest in Christ. It is beyond human art and means to make them at all solicitous about this great salvation, though they know that their eternal welfare depends upon it.

And what can be the reason that this madness is in the hearts of men? Can condemned, perishing sinners be unconcerned about the only method of escape from eternal damnation? Can they set more value by their lusts and pleasures, by the world and its vanities, and even by the merest trifles imaginable, than by Christ and his saving benefits? Can they rather choose to perish eternally, and to lose all the glories of the heavenly world, than to come to Christ that they might have life? As astonishing as this conduct appears, it is visibly the case of the world of mankind in general. And what reason can possibly be imagined of such unparalleled stupidity but this, that they have not (they cannot have, while under the power of a blind and carnal mind) any realizing view of this great concern? Could they but see their case as it is, a condemned malefactor could as easily set light by a pardon, or a drowning man by deliverance, as these perishing sinners by an offered Saviour.

We accordingly find that, when the Spirit of God comes upon them with his illuminations and opens their eyes to see their misery and impotency, they can be no longer careless about an interest in Christ. They can no longer make excuses and 'go their own way, one to his farm, and another to his merchandise' (Matt. 22:5). They can no longer amuse themselves with divers lusts and pleasures, and forget their necessity of Christ and his salvation. No! They have now nothing so much at heart as securing an interest in this blessed Saviour. Now this thought lies down and rises with them: 'What must I do to be saved? How shall I obtain an interest in Christ?' Now their distressed souls are groaning out these pathetic desires: 'Oh, for an interest in Christ! Let me have Christ, whatever I want!' The world now, with all its blandishments, all its riches and glory, dwindles to nothing in the eyes of a such humbled sinner, when compared with this excellent and needed Saviour. I may appeal to everyone that has been truly converted to God, at an age of observation, whether they have not experienced these things in their own hearts.

And, indeed, these operations of the mind are so rational that it would be considered impossible that we should neglect a most active concern about an interest in Christ, if the eyes of our understanding were enlightened. But alas! 'The light shines in darkness, and the darkness comprehendeth it not' (John 1:5). We see by experience that men never do (never will) show themselves thoroughly in earnest about this everlasting concern till the Spirit of God open their eyes and turn them from darkness to light, and that when they are thus illuminated they cannot do otherwise. This wonderful change in men's desires and pursuits is a necessary consequence of divine illumination and of a just and reasonable view of things. Without this, they cannot attain it; with this, they cannot fail of it. To this therefore the apostle ascribes it: 'For God, who commanded the light to shine out of darkness, hath shined in our hearts, to give the light of the knowledge of the glory of God in the face of Jesus Christ' (2 Cor. 4:6).

4. In the same manner also is the actual conversion of a sinner accomplished. In order to do this, the Spirit of God gives him *a realizing sight of the fulness and sufficiency that there is in Christ, and of his willingness and readiness to save him.*

The attainments before described do not necessarily imply a saving conversion to God. Though these are the influences of the blessed Spirit, they are not his special and saving operations. The sinner is not brought into a state of favour with God till he accepts a tendered Saviour upon his own terms. It is by receiving him that we have power to become the sons of God. The first act of saving faith is that conversion by which the sinner effectually turns from sin to God, passes from death to life, and becomes interested in Christ and all his saving benefits.

Now, which way is the sinner brought to this, but by an impressed, lively discovery of things as they are? By a lively sight of his sin and danger, powerfully applied to his mind and conscience, and appearing as it is, he is awakened to an earnest enquiry after the way of salvation. By a clear discovery of his unworthiness and impotence, he is brought to the footstool of God's sovereignty, and to an earnest desire of an interest in Christ, as I observed before.

But here the soul is often plunged into greatest darkness and distress: his guilt stares him in the face; he sees he has no claim to mercy, nothing that can entitle him to it. He has been struggling in vain to mortify his corruptions, to enliven his affections and to do something to recommend himself to God's favour, and is now perhaps ready to give up the case as helpless and hopeless. He cannot see how God can have mercy upon such a guilty, polluted, hard-hearted, hellish sinner as he is. Propose to him the only remedy for such lost sinners, and how many objections will be in the way! How many arguments will he bring against believing in Christ: from his own unworthiness and want of qualifications to come to him; from the decrees of God; from his having sinned away the day of grace, and the like — even till he runs into despair, unless the Spirit of God disperse the dark cloud, and give him a right view of redeeming mercy!

But when once such a distressed soul sees this as it is, when once he has an impressed sense of gospel grace and is brought to see indeed that he is invited to come to Christ, notwithstanding all his guilt and unworthiness, and that this precious Saviour is able and willing to bestow all that salvation upon him which he stands in need of — then his objections are silenced, and he cannot refrain from heartily complying with the offer. Then he can commit his soul to him, for he sees that there is utmost safety in doing so. Then he can depend upon him as the Author of his eternal salvation, for he sees that he has nowhere else to go, and that Christ has the words of eternal life.

It is remarkable that the Scriptures everywhere annex salvation to faith, and to the belief of the truth; and we are told, 'Whosoever believeth that Jesus is the Christ is born of God' (1 John 5:1). But what are we to understand by this belief? Will a cold and inactive assent to this truth interest us in Christ and his salvation? No! 'Faith is the substance of things hoped for, the evidence of things not seen' (Heb. 11:1). In which is more than a bare assent implied. It implies such a realizing view as makes all the offers of salvation by Christ certain, and his purchased benefits present to the believer.

And when a weary and heavy-laden soul has such a sight of the fulness and sufficiency, of the kindness and com-passion of Christ, and of his willingness to save him upon his coming to him, as makes this comfortable truth, as it were, personally present to his mind, when he has such a view that this Saviour is offered freely to him, without money and without price, it is impossible for him to do otherwise than consent to such reasonable terms of salvation. How can he refuse his consent to these terms, when his distress of soul had before prepared him for a compliance with any terms of obtaining God's favour? It is impossible for him to do otherwise than set the highest value by such a Saviour, when he has this sight — that grace here, and glory hereafter, is implied in his interest in Christ. It is impossible for him to do otherwise than have his dependence upon Christ only when he has this sight, that in him all fulness dwells, and that there is no safety anywhere else.

But I hope (if God will) more particularly to describe a true, saving faith. I am now only endeavouring to show that the Spirit of God works this grace in us by illuminating our minds and giving us a right exercise of our understandings.

5. The Spirit of God does likewise carry on the work of grace in a believer's sanctification *by continued views of spiritual things as they are.* By faith, the soul is united to the Lord Jesus Christ, and becomes one spirit with him. By faith, believers have an interest in all the benefits of Christ's redemption. They have thereby a claim to all the promises of the covenant of grace, and may safely and confidently depend upon the faithfulness of God, that he will give them grace and glory; that they shall be kept by his power, through faith, unto salvation; that 'he who hath begun a good work in them will perform it unto the day of Jesus Christ' (Phil. 1:6); that he who 'spared not his own Son, but delivered him up for them all, will with him also freely give them all things' (Rom. 8:32); and that upon their believing in Christ, out of their bellies 'shall flow rivers of living water' (John 7:38).

And what way is this glorious work of grace carried on in the soul, but by the continued assistances of the blessed Spirit to act reasonably, and to maintain a lively apprehension and impression of invisible realities? How does the believer come to hate every false way, but by a lively view of the vileness and unreasonableness of sinning against God? What excites him to live in the love of God, but a realizing impression of the excellency of God's nature, the infinite value of his favour, and the endearing attractiveness of his goodness, kindness and compassion? What makes him in love with holiness, but a sensible discovery of its internal beauty and agreeableness to a reasonable being? How comes he weaned from the world, but by a true sight of its vanity, and utter insufficiency to satisfy the desires of an immortal nature? How come his affections to be placed upon the things above, but from a like discovery of the value and importance of things unseen and eternal? What is communion with God, but a just impression of what pertains to God and godliness? And what are the evidences of God's favour, but a realization of the acts of grace in our souls, and of the truth of the invitations and promises of the gospel? The extraordinary influences of the Spirit in his immediate communications of light and joy to the believer are but still a brighter discovery of things as they are.

In a word, in whatever aspect this case in considered, what I am pleading for will (I think) appear to be truth. The whole work of sanctification is carried on by illumination and by the soul's being brought, through the influences of God's Spirit, to the exercise of knowledge and understanding; and to this the apostle ascribes it:

> That the God of our Lord Jesus Christ, the Father of glory, may give unto you the Spirit of wisdom and revelation in the knowledge of him: the eyes of your understanding being enlightened; that ye may know what is the hope of his calling, and what the riches of the glory of his inheritance in the saints (Eph. 1:17–18).

Upon the whole, I cannot see that the Spirit of God does in any other manner work this wonderful change in the hearts of sinners, than by giving them a just view of things as they are, by bringing them to act reasonably, worthy the dignity of their rational nature, and the intellectual powers they are endowed with. By this he conquers the enmity to

God that there is in their hearts, and brings them from the power of their lusts, of Satan and the world, into the fear and favour of God. By opening their eyes, he turns them from darkness to light, and from the power of Satan unto God, that they may have an inheritance among those that are sanctified.

If it be objected that the will must be changed and renewed, as well as the understanding enlightened, in the conversion of a sinner, that the Spirit of God works in us both to will and to do of his good pleasure, and Christ's people must be made willing in the day of his power, this is readily granted. But the question is, in what manner is the will changed, and how does the Lord Jesus Christ bring the stubborn, obdurate will of the sinner into subjection to himself? To this I answer as before: by giving them a realizing, affecting sight of things as they are. It is impossible for a reasonable being to do otherwise than what appears to be, in all circumstances, best for him and most agreeable and desirable to him. Did therefore carnally secure sinners see things as they are, did they realize to themselves the folly and danger of their lusts, the misery of an unconverted state, their need of a Saviour and the excellency of Christ, the advantage of an interest in him, the benefits of a life of religion with respect both to this world and that to come? I say, if they saw these things in a just and powerful light, their wills would necessarily be changed. They would no longer choose the way of destruction and death, before the path of life and peace. They would no longer venture eternal damnation, rather than accept of happiness here and for ever.

We are not therefore to suppose that the Spirit of God properly puts any force upon men's inclinations, when he changes their wills. The will is not violated. He does but give them a true discovery, a realizing view and powerful impression of what is best for them, and that necessarily determines their choice. Let sinners, if they can, be willing to rush upon the pikes of God's displeasure, when the Spirit by strong convictions and illuminations gives them a full and clear sight of their sins and of the flaming vengeance that hangs over their guilty heads. Let them, if they can, refuse a tendered Saviour, when they are brought to see their extreme necessity of him, with his fulness, sufficiency and readiness to save them. Or let them, if they can, choose the service of sin and Satan before the service of God, when they have a feeling sense of the danger and misery of the one, and the excellency, desirableness and safety of the other.

In a word, though men may have the greatest degree of doctrinal knowledge, in the things now treated of, understand them well, discourse of them rationally and articulately and receive them for truth, without any change of their wills and affections, yet if through the Spirit they had any lively and affecting apprehension of these unseen and eternal concerns, they must of necessity have an influence upon their hearts and lives, proportionate to the kind and degree of the light impressed on their minds. Though a academic knowledge of these things will serve no other purpose but to leave the sinner the more inexcusable, yet when the Spirit of God sets them home with power upon the soul, in their own proper light and evidence, this prospect cannot fail to have a blessed effect.

APPENDIX II
THE CONVERSION OF
C. H. SPURGEON
(IN HIS OWN WORDS)

I had been about five years in the most fearful distress of mind, as a lad. If any human being felt more of the terror of God's law, I can indeed pity and sympathize with him. [John] Bunyan's *Grace Abounding* contains, in the main, my history. Some abysses he went into, I never trod, but some into which I plunged, he seems to have never known.

I thought the sun was blotted out of my sky — that I had sinned so against God that there was no hope for me. I prayed — the Lord knoweth how I prayed; but I never had a glimpse of an answer that I knew of. I searched the Word of God; the promises were more alarming than the threatenings. I read the privileges of the people of God, but with the fullest persuasion that they were not for me. The secret of my distress was this: I did not know the gospel. I was in a Christian land; I had Christian parents; but I did not fully understand the freeness and simplicity of the gospel.

I attended all the places of worship in the town where I lived, but I honestly believe that I did not hear the gospel fully preached. I do not blame the men, however. One man preached divine sovereignty. I could hear him with pleasure. But what was that to a poor sinner who wished to know what he should do to be saved? There was another admirable man who always preached about the Law; but what was the use of ploughing up ground that wanted to be sown? Another was a great practical preacher. I heard him, but it was very much like a commanding officer teaching the manoeuvres of war to a set of men without feet. What could I do? All his exhortations were lost to me. I knew it was said, 'Believe on the Lord Jesus Christ and thou shall be saved', but I did not know what it was to believe in Christ.

I sometimes think I might have been in darkness and despair now had it not been for the goodness of God in sending a snowstorm one Sunday morning, when I was going to a place of worship. When I could go no further, I turned down a court and came to a little Primitive Methodist chapel. In that chapel there might be a dozen or fifteen people. The minister did not come that morning; snowed up, I suppose. A poor man, a shoemaker, a tailor, or something of that sort, went up into the pulpit to preach.

Now, it is well that ministers should be instructed, but this man was really stupid, as you would say. He was obliged to stick to his text, for the simple reason he had nothing else to say. The text was, 'Look unto me, and be ye saved, all the ends of the earth' [Isa. 45:22]. He did not even pronounce the words rightly, but that did not matter.

There was, I thought, a glimpse of hope for me in that text. He began thus: 'My dear friends, this is a very simple text indeed. It says, "Look." Now, that does not take a great deal of effort. It ain't lifting your foot or your finger. It is just "Look." Well, a man need not go to college to learn to look. A man need not be worth a thousand a year to look. Anyone can look; a child can look. But this is what the text says. Then it says, "Look *unto me*."'

'Aye,' said he, in broad Essex, 'many of ye are looking to yourselves. No use looking there. You'll never find comfort in yourselves. Some look to God the Father. No, look to him by and by. Jesus Christ says, "Look unto me." Some of you say, "I must wait the Spirit's working." You have no business with that just now. "Look to Christ." It runs: "Look unto me."'

Then the good man followed up his text in this way: 'Look unto me; I am sweating great drops of blood. Look unto me; I am hanging on the cross. Look! I am dead and buried. Look unto me; I rise again. Look unto me; I ascend; I am sitting at the Father's right hand. Oh, look unto me! Look unto me!'

When he had got about that length, and managed to spin out ten minutes or so, he was at the length of his tether. Then he looked at me under the gallery, and I dare say, with so few present, he knew me to be a stranger. He then said, 'Young man, you look very miserable.' Well, I did; but I had not been accustomed to have remarks made on my personal appearance from the pulpit before. However, it was a good blow struck. He continued: 'And you will always be miserable — miserable in life, and miserable in death — if you do not obey my text. But if you obey now, this moment you will be saved.'

Then he shouted, as only a Primitive Methodist can, 'Young man, look to Jesus Christ!' I did 'look'. There and then, the cloud was gone, the darkness had rolled away, and that moment I saw the sun; I could have risen that moment and sung with the most enthusiastic of them of the precious blood of Christ, and the simple faith which looks alone to him. Oh, that somebody had told me that before: 'Trust Christ, and you shall be saved.'

It was, no doubt, wisely ordered, and I must ever say:

E'er since by faith I saw the stream
Thy wounds supplied for me,
Redeeming love has been my theme,
And shall for ever be.

APPENDIX III: RESPONSES FROM READERS OF THE FIRST EDITION

In the introduction I alluded to a few responses from the first edition of this book. Most contacts were by telephone or email; some were direct personal conversations and 'snail mail'. I wish now I had kept all the written correspondence and emails, but some survived and portions of these (slightly edited) are quoted below.

Via email — 26 June 1998
I've just been reading your book *Are you really born again?* and it has had such an impact on me that I had to write to you. I'm the pastor of an Apostolic Church in Singapore. It is a small church of fifty and we are primarily reaching out to Indians and Malays in Singapore, the least evangelized groups in Singapore. We are under the Apostolic denomination, which is Pentecostal. And we are trinitarian. I have

spent time analyzing my own conversion, and I'm thinking through everything I've done in church. I have tears in my eyes as I wonder how many of my people are truly on their way to heaven. There are only two choices — life or death. This Sunday I'm going to get all my members to hand in a written testimony in one week on how and why they became a Christian. Then I'm going to follow-up on each person one-to-one.

Via email — 13 September 1998
I am writing to you to thank you for your book *Are you really born again?* The book came to me during a period in which I was deeply depressed, one in which I felt estranged from God and was struggling to get back to him. I was disillusioned with other Christians, the church and with everything in general.

I bought your book at a local bookstore (I live in England), believing it would confirm my suspicions about myself — namely that I had never been converted and I had been 'fooling myself'.

On the contrary, the chapters 'Sings of the unconverted', 'True conversion' and 'Profiles of true and false conversion' reaffirmed my belief in my own saved state. I examined myself deeply and realized that I do have an assurance of salvation.

Via email — 12 October 1998
Let me start by saying how much I enjoyed reading the book. I'm a sixty-one-year-old elder and with all the books I've read, no one has ever stated clearly the mystery surrounding the new birth as you have. It has given me a feeling of release when I am preaching or sharing the gospel. It is comforting to know that we can only be faithful in presenting the message of man's complete ruin and Christ's complete work, and leave the rest up to the Spirit of God.

I have struggled over exactly what it means to believe and always came up short when trying to explain it. One area I still personally have a problem with is assurance. I have always understood that to be accomplished through the Word of God and not through any emotional or physical experience. I suppose that assurance will come by faith in God's Word. That is, as I am able to accept by faith what God through Christ has done, my assurance will be there.

Via email — 5 May 1998
I am a church-based evangelist with a UK evangelical church. I enjoyed reading your book *Are you really born again?* and you have come to the same conclusions that I have about appeals at the end of an evangelistic talk. It is something that I have wrestled with for years and since I began using my own way of ending a talk rather than copying the standard methods I am much more at peace with my ministry.

I read the whole of John Wesley's *Journal* (all 4 volumes) and could not find one time when Wesley led the congregation in a sinner's prayer. This troubled me and I now know that it is vital for us to be co-workers with the Holy Spirit as evangelists and that we must steer people to Jesus and let the Holy Spirit do his work of convicting of sin, righteousness and judgement.

After preaching Christ and him crucified I explain that people must confess their sin to Jesus, repent and declare him as their living Lord and Saviour. I have a moment of silence so that they can pray to the Lord in their own words. I have always found this a precious time and it is plain to see a wrestling with the Spirit as some respond to him.

In a prison this last Sunday 114 prisoners were silent for many minutes and I could see that some were really engaged in prayer. Twenty inmates asked for an application to see the chaplain and he can now see what has happened in their lives, begin discipleship and look for the fruits of repentance.

I believe the Puritans had a name for a false conversion — it was called 'false peace' and they taught it a lot.

Thank you once again for your book. I will commend it to any pastor or evangelist.

Via email — 20 April 1998
I've just completed your book. It's good reading and timely. How true it is that there are many who believe that all is well with their soul while they dance on the brink of hell. My conversion experience was similar to yours and I thank God for it — although at the time it was difficult. Deep conviction of sin for about nine months and then at a Baptist gathering (I'm Presbyterian of the conservative kind) the truth of salvation burst upon my soul. I knew it all before in my head, but then the truth burst on my heart. I just thank God for his abundant mercy.

Undated
I just wanted to thank you for *Are you really born again?* which I am reading. The matters dealt with are crucial and I pray that the book will be a great help to saints and sinners alike. I have tried to deal with the issue on several occasions in print and many times in preaching so I am truly with you in your aim.

Via email — 1 February 2000
I like the way you address the two truths of the mystery of conversion. You called it a paradox. I have had in-depth conversations with a friend and he called it an 'antinomy'. The dictionary says an antinomy is a contradiction between two seemingly true statements. Our pastor has addressed the issue and he says the Bible presents both truths side by side and that is just where we should leave them (exactly what you did).

21 October 2001

I bought your book with great interest because I believe my wife is not born again, although she sincerely believes that she is. I know you will agree that God is the ultimate Judge of who is and who is not born again. And yet, in his Word, as you have pointed out in your book, he has given us evidences of true conversion. ...

I felt led to write to you, upon your invitation, to share another type of unsaved individual that I didn't quite see in your book. In your tenth chapter, 'Signs of the unconverted', under the heading 'The religious "Christian" unconverted' I believe there could be another sub-heading called 'The deceived'. The people in this group, in general, believe the *right* things. This is the part that I feel needs to be stressed. There are multitudes of people in the professing church who in the main have *correct* theologies, who truly do believe the right things; they are well taught, but it is only cerebral. They went through the 'formula' presented to them for becoming a Christian, and after they prayed the prayer they were told by a well-meaning counsellor that they were now Christians. I agree with you that many are saved going through the 'formula'. But sadly, many are not. Then they are told that they are now Christians and to never doubt it. These deceived people are very hard to reach. They lack the evidences in their lives, but they get angry if you seek to confront them because they prayed to receive Christ, and they protest, 'the Bible says if we pray that, we are saved'. The problem with so many of these deceived people is they have little or no fruit in their lives to validate their profession. They are assured, and blindly content, that they are 'OK' because they 'accepted Christ' at some point in time.

You make mention throughout your book of the long-standing practice in the church of accepting anyone into the fellowship who repeats the sinner's prayer. How very true! And this is exactly where I believe my dear wife is today. There are many others in the church just like her.

EPILOGUE

Some readers may want to write the author — with questions, to make suggestions, to offer anecdotes from their own experience or to discuss certain points from *Are you really born again?* We welcome your feedback and comments.

You can email Kent Philpott at:
    kentphilpott@comcast.net

Or visit the Miller Avenue Baptist Church website:
    www.w3church.org